Global Passion

Global Passion

Marking George Verwer's Contribution to World Missions

David Greenlee

editor

Peter Conlan, Greg Kernaghan, Peter Maiden
associate editors

Authentic
LIFESTYLE

First published in 2003 by Authentic Lifestyle
Reprinted 2004

10 09 08 07 06 05 04   8 7 6 5 4 3 2
Authentic Lifestyle is an imprint of Authentic Media,
PO Box 300, Carlisle, Cumbria, CA3 0QS, UK
and PO Box 1047, Waynesboro, GA 30830-2047
www.authenticmedia.co.uk

British Library Cataloguing in Publication Data

A catalogue record for this book is available from
the British Library

ISBN 1-85078-528-7

Cover design by David Lund
Printed in Great Britain by
Bell and Bain Ltd. Glasgow

Contents

Section 3
The Greatest Missions Movement in History 93

Section 4 Word of Tribute

George Verwer

Revolutionary Realist
Compassionate Visionary
Passionate Servant
Grabber of the Impossible
Friend of Failures

For your
Christ-centered life
inspiring leadership
transparent integrity
irrepressible humour
and
gracious zeal

We present these essays in appreciation
for the volumes you have written
into our lives
and the lives of countless others

All to the glory of God.

Gratitude For a Life Well Lived

Peter Maiden

Well, George, you've made it to sixty-five! I've listened to dark prophecies for many years. 'He'll never make it to sixty; the pace he lives is bound to catch up with him!' And you've certainly lived at an incredible pace. I for one have been breathless at times trying to keep up with you. But the chapters which follow will show that your life is not just speed but a life leading to concrete achievements for the glory of God. These achievements have been immense and extremely diverse.

One Passion, Many Proofs

Some pioneer change agents hold the sniper's rifle. You have held the blunderbuss! What one thing do we remember about these past forty years of leadership? Will it be your impact on the growth of short-term missions? OM must have been one of the first groups to develop this whole idea. It has of course become a major means of providing opportunities for people to test whether they have the calling and the capacity for longer-term service. Short-termers have also planted churches and done incredible work in their own right. Now every major missionary society I come across has their short-term programme.

Will it be your commitment to literature – STL and the subsequent Wesley Owen chain in the UK, OM Literature in the States, the massive literature ministry in India? Your promotion and funding of titles all over the world? Your incredible book-tables which have provided free and immensely cheap Christian books to tens of thousands?

Will the contribution remembered be your perseverance in prayer? So many OMers I meet refer back to their first half-night of prayer as a life-transforming experience. The way you've committed yourself to that weekly half-night of prayer has been an immense personal challenge to me.

Will it be the mobilization of people into missions? Only eternity will reveal the number of people who moved into mission because of your example, your preaching, your prayers, your books. What is more, they have been people of all ages and a variety of gift-ings. You have shown that missions is not a specialist occupation. You have helped many into a lifetime of missions service who would not have been accepted by traditional missionary agencies.

Will your contribution be in the globalization of missions? I am convinced that OM is now one of the most globalized mission agencies on earth because of strategies that you implemented in the early days and your example. That globalized mission force certainly makes OM a most exciting, refreshing and challenging movement to be part of.

Or will it be your commitment to tens of thousands of individuals? George, I'm amazed as I travel to discover how many people with whom you're in written or telephone communication. And I know it's not just the great and the good. There are so many out there who – when they have been struggling – have found you to be, as Greg Livingstone wrote in a personal tribute, 'a true friend'.

You have lived at an amazing pace and made a multitude of contributions to the work of the Kingdom. And yet at sixty-five you seem to be going as strong as ever. I for one hope and pray that you'll continue to go strong for many years to come. What has been the secret of your continuing energy and motivation?

One thing I really appreciate is your understanding that this is 'His work'. You certainly give everything you've got to the work. But you've always had that ability to 'leave it with the Lord'. I've been with you on many occasions when you've been under the burden of a multitude of pressures. But you've always seemed to be able to 'leave it with Him' – when necessary, to walk away from the pressures and enjoy nine holes of golf (Eighteen holes you've always found to be over-indulgent). You've always been able to play or relax as hard as you work. The advent of the mobile phone has of course made golf even more enjoyable for you! Etched in my mind are issues we've discussed just after you've driven off from the third or the seventh hole!

Mr. Natural

Your ability to be yourself has also been a key to your survival. You're not terrorised by the expectations of others. I remember sitting with one of my co-editors of this book and one of your close friends, Peter Conlan. We were in the front row of a large auditorium in Birmingham. We along with others had organized a national conference for about 1,000 young Christian leaders. We'd spent many months organizing this weekend around the theme of the leader as a soldier. The talks were to be taken from 2 Timothy. We other speakers had spent many hours preparing our talks on Chapters 1, 2 and 4. You had the third session to be based on Chapter 3. You'd flown in overnight to London from Pakistan; when you arrived in Birmingham it was obvious you were pretty wrecked. You got onto the platform and began speaking. You were presenting books and making comments on your recent trip. You normally start your sermons this way, but the introduction went on longer than usual. All the time you were flicking back and forward through your Bible. After a few minutes, Peter turned to me and said, 'I think we're in trouble.' Eventually to everyone's amazement you said in a jet-lagged voice, 'I can't find 2 Timothy, Acts is a bigger book, we'll speak tonight from that.' I think other Christian leaders more concerned with image than you would have tried to find some other way out of the dilemma!

A couple of years ago I was preaching in a church in South Korea. You'd preached at the church twelve months previously. I was told on a number of occasions of the strict dress code that would be required and I did my best to conform. As a matter of interest I spoke to the pastor after preaching. 'When George was here twelve months ago did he wear a suit and tie?' But of course not; you'd worn your famous global jacket.

This willingness to be yourself, to be seen as you are 'warts and all' takes much pressure off you. It's also been a great encouragement to me and many others. We've been challenged to think, 'It's possible: God can even use us with all our weakness and failings.' I know tens of thousands of young people have been and still are being challenged and encouraged by the personal examples in your preaching of what Ajith Fernando in his contribution to this book calls, 'life in the raw.'

You are not a perfectionist, George – another reason why you've been able to achieve so much and stay sane. David Greenlee recalls your comment in his contribution, that 'faith doesn't just have Plan A and Plan B but X, Y and Z as well.' That's typical of you. You're a sensible pragmatist as well as a man of faith and prayer. This has meant amongst other things that you've never been too proud to admit when you're wrong.

You've had to reassess things which have been fundamental to your thinking and over time ultimately come to a different position. My mind goes back to a moving leaders' meeting when the issue of our financial policy was raised. OM was known around the world for our policy of only mentioning financial needs when the initiative was taken by someone to ask us. We were looking at some very difficult situations in which this policy just did not appear to be working. You left the meeting, went away to a farm to which you like to retreat to from time to time and took the whole thing before the Lord. The result was a brand new proposal which presented a very significant change of policy. Your willingness to change at that point and not to hold on to the past – even to principles important to us – has been immensely important for this movement.

This capacity to acknowledge that things have not always been right and therefore to change your position or that things may have been right for a time but now a new time has come, has been crucial to your own survival and to the development of OM. This pragmatism and willingness to change probably saved OM in the earlier days from slipping into real extremism and consequent marginalization.

However, you would be the first to agree that there's one person apart from the Lord Jesus who has been vital in all that you've achieved and are today: Drena. No appreciation of you, George, would be complete without equal appreciation of her. In the light of that, you may remember a visit to your home when I gave some vague reason for interviewing Drena. It was actually for this book!

Interview with Drena Verwer, 27 September, 2002

Peter: Drena, when and where did you first set eyes on George?
Drena: In 1959, when I was a secretary at Moody Bible Institute.

Peter: And your first thought when you set eyes on him?
Drena: I thought he came from the back woods!

Peter: How did things develop from there?
Drena: I read an article about him in the school newspaper. He was going to lead some kind of mission and I thought, 'Well, he's a student. How can he do that at the same time?' So I offered my secretarial help. He later told me that he thought I was flirting with him!

Peter: While at Moody you yourself were already moving towards mission?
Drena: Yes, definitely. It was simultaneous: when I got saved, I knew the Lord was calling me to the mission field.

Peter: At that point did you have any specific idea as to where God was leading you?
Drena: No. I knew I had to have Bible college training first. Moody Bible College was the only place I'd heard of and so there I was, working as a secretary to get into school to start my training. Mission for me was the African jungle. It was the only thing I knew about mission.

Peter: How did it progress from George thinking you were flirting with him to a relationship beginning?
Drena: I told him I wanted to help in any way. He asked if I would go on visitation with him to a Spanish-speaking area of the city. I didn't know a word of Spanish. So I went with him and his Spanish teacher. After that he wanted me to go through the book

of Acts with him so we did that instead of proper dating. Things developed from there.

Peter: How long after you first met George were you married?

Drena: It was over a year, because Moody had a rule that if a student gets married in the middle of their education they have to drop out for a year before coming back and finishing. George was not going to delay getting to the mission field, so we started dating after three months and then we got engaged for just over a year. We married the week after George graduated.

Peter: There are some crazy stories about the early days, like George selling things which were part of your wedding. How much of it is true?

Drena: The stories are probably about our wedding cake. When we got married we asked for no gifts. If people wanted to give, they had to give us money because we said we were going to be doing a lot of travelling. Mexico and Spain were the places we had in mind. Our wedding reception was a potluck lunch which the church gave us as our wedding gift. We actually had two wedding cakes. One, which I didn't get a bite of, was large. A smaller cake was there because we were concerned there wouldn't be enough to go round. It was the smaller wedding cake – eventually unused – that got us from Chicago to Mexico City! We left for Mexico right after the wedding and George drove as far as he could. When we got low on petrol, we'd start at the entrance to the city and visit all the petrol stations. We would explain that we were just married and on our way to Mexico as missionaries. We asked if we could exchange our wedding cake for a tank of fuel. The first three times, people were either sympathetic to us or may have been committed Christians and they gave us a free tank of fuel and let us keep the cake. Eventually we hit another fuel station and a man took our cake in exchange for the petrol. That's how we got to Mexico!

Peter: From Mexico you went straight to Spain?

Drena: More or less. We were six months in Mexico from January to June. The next group of students from the United States came for the summer campaign in Mexico. We met them at the border and had our training conference. After that we left for Spain, arriving in September.

Peter: Over the last forty years you've lived in Spain, Nepal, India, Britain…where else?

Drena: We've lived on the ships, Italy, France and I'm sure other places as well.

Peter: But you don't like travelling?

Drena: I actually hate travelling. Ever since I can remember, even before I met George, I've just wanted to stay in one place.

Peter: As you think back over life with George these last forty years, mention one or two qualities of George that really stand out for you.

Drena: When I first started to meet with George, I was also going out with two other people from Moody.

Peter: Now I'm beginning to understand where the OM social policy came from!

Drena: But the one thing that drew me to George was his godliness. I saw God in George and I felt I needed someone strong enough to be my leader. George fitted that bill for me. I also trust his judgement and his decisions. That doesn't mean I've always submitted easily.

Peter: There must be some weaknesses, Drena. What frustrates you about George?

Drena: He's very intense, always active, and can't sit down for more than a few minutes. He's absolutely useless at small talk! As you can see, we live in a paper jungle; my whole house constantly looks like a paper warehouse!

Peter: Do you ever wish you'd married a man who had a nice quiet job leaving home at 9am and getting back at 5pm, maybe in a country village with a nice local church which you could visit on a Sunday morning at 11am. Do you ever wish for a life like that?

Drena: Well, maybe I have from time to time – but then I stop and think and I know I've married the right man and chosen the right life.

Peter: As you think of the transition that George is making, what are your concerns – for him, for the movement, for yourself?

Drena: George is going to cope OK because he's already got so many things on his mind that he wants to do. I probably think I'll struggle with it more than George. I feel I know George's mind. I know the decisions that he would make. I think I'll struggle with the fact that inevitably the new leadership won't necessarily do what I think George would have done.

Peter: Do you have any concerns for the movement at this stage?

Drena: Well, I hope it won't change too much. I hope it's going to stay on the cutting edge and I hope the prayer life will stay priority. That's my biggest concern.

Peter: Drena, I've always felt that you don't like the limelight.

Drena: You're absolutely right. I find it extremely difficult when I'm dragged into the limelight. For these past forty years all I've ever wanted is to support George. If I could have done that without being seen I would have loved it.

Peter: Thanks Drena for all you've done and for all you mean to us in OM.

You Will Always Lead

George, that's another contribution you two have undoubtedly made. You've been very open about struggles within your marriage but the absolute commitment of both of you to being the best that you can be as husband and wife – especially in today's world – has been a vital example to many.

On behalf of the whole movement and the hundreds of thousands of friends of OM around the world, thank you for your inspiring and honest leadership of OM. I'm extremely grateful that you'll continue to labour with us within this movement. On behalf of us all, I give the following commitment:

The values that we have embraced as OM internationally will continue to be at the heart of everything we are and we seek to do.

- Knowing and glorifying God
- Living in submission to His Word
- Being people of grace and integrity
- Serving sacrificially
- Loving and valuing people
- Reflecting the diversity of the body of Christ
- Evangelizing the world
- Global intercession
- Esteeming the church

I know you'll keep praying for us to 'stay on track' and I'll be very surprised if we don't get the occasional word of exhortation!

Peter Maiden has been designated as Operation Mobilisation's International Co-ordinator as of August 2003. Peter also serves as an elder in his local church, is Co-chairman of the International Christian College in Glasgow, and Chairman of the Keswick Convention. Along with this he keeps busy with an intensive Bible teaching ministry throughout Britain and in many other countries of the world. A voracious reader, he is an avid long-distance runner, often in the fells of the English Lake District. Peter resides in Carlisle with his wife, Win. They have three married children and two grandchildren.

The Lordship of Christ[1]

George Verwer

I remember this meeting in Germany. I was going on about an hour and a half; the young people seemed to be listening but someone way up in the back wanted me to stop so he held up his wristwatch. I was preaching about world missions, discipleship and giving your all for Christ. I saw this watch and I said, 'Oh praise the Lord. Look at this man! He's donating his watch for missionary work!' I can assure you that InterVarsity USA has more effective methods than that.

I thought I was going to become completely unglued last night when I met Billy Graham. He's my spiritual father. I'd never met him. I've read his books and listened to his tapes. His Urbana '57 tape I've listened to over fifteen times. That was required listening for everyone who came into Operation Mobilisation for many years. I got overdosed on Billy Graham; I read so many books and tapes I started to have Billy Graham dreams, Billy Graham nightmares; I was wanting to meet him and I wasn't wanting to meet him – then suddenly he was there in that room. I had a minute for each ten years since that time thirty-two years ago. Praise the Lord I'm still here.

Some of you stood up last night and made this decision. Maybe you were like me: I didn't understand it. I was from a nominal Christian home. I actually brought binoculars to that meeting in Madison Square Garden because I'd heard he was a hypnotist and I wanted to see what he was doing. He preached a very basic message

as he did last night. And in fear and trembling I trusted the Lord
Jesus Christ. The psychology books tell us that's a late adolescent
escape from guilt. Many people say it doesn't last but I can tell you
that what happened to me in Madison Square Garden thirty-two
years ago has been a precious reality every single day ever since. Jesus
is real!

Turn with me in your Bibles to the most important commandment in all of Scripture. We are living in a day of mega-
information and I find that many people are confused and have
misplaced priorities. We have a lot of people majoring on minors.
I want to deal with some of the most basic issues in our entire
Christian faith this evening.

As our text we are taking Mark 12:30, 31: 'And thou shalt love
the Lord thy God with all thy heart, with all thy soul, with all thy
mind and with all thy strength. This is the first commandment.'
With all the other emphases, all the books, all the tapes – we no
longer have book worms in OM, we have a whole army of tape
worms. Incredible! – let's remember this: 'Thou shalt love the
Lord thy God with all thy heart, with all thy soul, with all thy
mind, and all thy strength. This is the first commandment and the
second is like namely this: thou shalt love thy neighbour as thyself.
There is none other commandment greater than these.'

I have wrestled with this message on the lordship of Christ
more than almost any other. As I was wrestling with this, praying,
reading books and listening to tapes, seven words came into my
heart. I know you're getting so many messages here, so many
words – how can you take notes? It's difficult, but I would like you
to write down these seven words and I pray that, if you look back
at my feeble message some years down the road, you'll remember
these seven words.

Lordship

We believe in the lordship of Jesus Christ. I was so challenged by
the presentation of IFES, one of the greatest spiritual missionary
movements in the world. We consider it a great privilege to have
a partnership with this great movement across the world. I have
the burden to see far more finance released for that great work. I

don't know if you can imagine how short-staffed and how weak that work is in some of the nations like Italy, a land very much on my heart. There is no time to speak of that but I hope you will get more information.

I'm sure most of the fellowships represented here believe in the lordship of Jesus Christ. It's amazing that Billy Graham has been criticized for a sort of an easy-believism. I've had people outside my meeting some time ago on the East Coast giving out very extreme literature about lordship and the idea that hardly anyone is saved except them. It's amazing how Satan can take any precious doctrine and try to get it into extremes. Brother or sister, if you begin to move for God in these days, if you made a commitment last night, if you make a commitment in these coming evenings, Satan is going to counterattack with two basic strategies. First of all, he wants to keep you from really knowing the fullness of the spirit, commitment and the lordship of Christ. Then, when you do begin to move in that reality, Satan will try to get you into extremism. (Beware of extremism and try to find a balance of Scripture.)

Another example is the famous cliché that says 'if Jesus Christ isn't Lord of all he isn't Lord at all'. When I heard that I thought, 'Boy, that's great. Let's thump people on the head with that one.' But then I asked, 'Is it biblical?' I am convinced that we can come to know Christ as Saviour in a moment. Some did last night. I did at Madison Square Garden at sixteen years of age, though I'd been prayed for by the real founder of our work: a dear, praying elderly lady who, when I was fifteen or fourteen, put me on her hit list. She prayed for me regularly. She sent me a Gospel of John through the mail. That Gospel of John prepared my heart and I ended up going to that Billy Graham meeting.

I believe you can come to know Jesus Christ in a second. But I believe that to know the Lordship of Jesus Christ in all that God wants that to mean in our lives takes a lifetime of constantly growing and repenting. Praise God that his blessed Holy Spirit doesn't reveal all the self-life to us in one glimpse. We wouldn't be able to handle the sight. But as we grow, as we get more in the word, as we get into various training experiences, God lovingly exposes our self and we repent and grow. We need a greater emphasis on spiritual growth. You may have a crisis experience in your life. You

may have a crisis this week. Hallelujah! I'm not against that –
though I personally have had too many – but if that crisis is not
followed by a process it will become an abscess.

Brothers and sisters, spiritual balance is not compromise, not
mixing the world with the church, not mixing truth and error.
Spiritual balance is taking one biblical truth and uniting it with
another major biblical truth. With all my heart, I believe it's the
only way to live.

Lordship. We need to ask ourselves the hard questions during
these days together. Is Jesus Christ really Lord of our lives? What
if we take just four categories of our lives?

Is the Lord Jesus Lord of our time?

A great man of God said, 'the greatest sin in America is wasting
time.' It just blows my mind the way people are investing their
time. Oftentimes people in the political arena, the sports arena, the
academic arena, even the arena of theatre and the arts are more
committed and disciplined than many of the evanjellyfish we have
swimming around today.

We need a little sanctified imagination. I know I got extreme
in the whole thing of redeeming time. Again it happened this
summer. I think the greatest invention since the printing press is
the Walkman. I got this at a discount for five dollars. You can put
on the Scriptures – I don't know what I have on here – Amy
Grant, no, New Testament! Put these earphones on and…this
summer my wife and I decided to take a little vacation and so I
put one ear for Scripture and I left the other ear for my wife as
we walked along! That got me into serious trouble.

But you know, I don't think extremism is the problem for most
of you. Forgive me if I'm wrong; you can write to me. I don't
know if you've read much of AW Tozer but I believe he is one of
the most laser beam writers that this country ever had. I hope
you'll read his books. Do you know what he said about worrying
about too much enthusiasm and extremism in an average church?
You know if that's a big problem in your church that people are
too excited about Christ, they're always running off witnessing,
they're neglecting the church supper. Is this the problem in your
church? Great, send me some photos, make a video! But I'll tell

you: AW Tozer said – and I'll never forget it – 'to think that too much enthusiasm was the greatest problem in the average church was like sending a squadron of policemen out to the nearby cemetery to guard against a demonstration by the residents!'

I find very few people today are memorizing Scripture. Many people acknowledge that they have lazy minds. Twenty years ago I gave an invitation here for people to repent and to enter into a radical life-changing walk with God. Four thousand people stood up at that invitation. I get letters from many of those people. I never wanted to write a book, but out of the Urbana convention came my book *Hunger for Reality*. I've received letters from people who've read that book – fifteen thousand and I've read all of them over twenty years. They have helped me to know what to say tonight. I'm indebted to those ordinary people all over the world who wrote to me in many languages and were willing to be honest.

I want to ask you to examine how you're using your time. I've been praying for a long time how to redeem the time more when I'm in a car. Sometimes vehicles don't have very good lights and it's hard to read. I hate to sit in the back of the car and not do something. Sometimes of course you can witness. Praise the Lord. For Christmas someone gave me these great glasses with lights! You can just read the word of God in the dark or wherever you go. Hallelujah! It's amazing.

You know it's good to laugh because sometimes the situation is so serious we either have to laugh or cry. Sometimes God uses humour and funny things in life to drive truth home. I pray you will seriously examine what you are doing with your time and that covers many other areas.

But is he also Lord over your tongue?

What about your mouth? This has been my problem. My mother wasn't a prophet but she said when I was small, 'Son, you've got a big mouth.' I've hardly had anyone compliment me about my mouth except once a dentist working on a back tooth said, 'There's plenty of space in here.'

If you are thinking about being a cross-cultural communicator then you must deal with the sins of the tongue. As a young baby Christian I read Billy Graham's sermon on 'The Sins of the

Tongue'. I repented and I cried to God and I said, 'Lord if you don't change my vocabulary, if you don't do something about my impatience and my irritability, I cannot serve you.' It was not until I got desperate in Mexico City after offending my young Mexican workers and repented and got into God's Word that I started to get more mouth control. Don't give up. If God can give victory and change a character like me, there's hope for everyone else.

Thirdly, is He Lord over your social life and emotions?

This, perhaps, is the biggest battle of all. In fact, Billy Graham in 1957 said that if you don't win the battle – this is a paraphrase but basically what he said – 'If you lose the battle against impurity you lose the battle of the Christian life.' I've been saying for twenty or more years that impurity is an epidemic in the church of Jesus Christ today and I tell you it scares me far more than AIDS.

I thank God for John White's book *Eros Defiled* and Erwin Lutzer's book *Living With your Passions*. Even if you have a slight struggle and problems in this area then you ought to get those books; you ought to memorize those chapters in Proverbs and look at the many other verses in the Bible on the subject of sex. In fact, there are over five hundred Scriptures about sex – even in the King James Version!

It's a great mistake if you think this battle is going to be immediately taken care of when you pray a nice prayer. I have battled my strong sexual drive all my life. I knew as a teenager it would make me or break me; that there was no middle ground. I had to be filled with the Spirit every day. I had to be crucified every day or I'd get in trouble. I'm a natural backslider. I'd go for sin like a grasshopper for wheat, if it wasn't for the power of Jesus Christ. And it isn't all victory.

I want you to know that we as Christian leaders are vulnerable and weak. We are strugglers. I had an experience even during a prayer walk. I live in London, England. I love to go in the woods and worship God. I often go for days of prayer. Here I was out in the woods praising and worshipping God and there was my old trouble – a pornographic magazine – hanging on a tree. I'm a pornoholic, just like an alcoholic: if I stay completely away, no problem. And there I was, walking in the woods, and that magazine was in the tree: a $10 magazine someone had used for target practice. What a wonderful testimony if I could stand in front of eighteen thousand people and tell you how George Verwer, the founder and leader of Operation Mobilisation, with one laser beam of power from the Holy Ghost zapped that magazine: pow! But the truth is that that magazine some years ago made a complete fool out of me.

And I tell you, I stand here not as 'the true disciple'. I stand here not as a Christian leader or as a public speaker or a spiritual revolutionary. I stand here as just a product of the grace of God. God uses ordinary people and I pray that you may understand though you may have struggles and feel that you're a failure. That failure can be the back door of success.

I had this great vision for the Soviet Union. I had no interest in Western Europe. I was learning Russian. I went into the Soviet Union. I got across the border with my printing press and my gospels in Corn Flakes boxes. Some of you know my good friend Brother Andrew, God's Smuggler. Tonight you've got Brother George, God's Bungler.

The second day in the Soviet Union, due to my own stupidity I was arrested by the secret police and accused of being a spy. A first-class fiasco. But I went back and spent the day in prayer near Vienna in the mountains. It was there that God gave me those two words – Operation Mobilisation – and the vision that European young people would be renewed, would mobilize and evangelize hundreds of millions across the world, reaching them with the gospel of Christ. And to some degree that has happened.

(There's a book out by Erwin Lutzer called *Failure, The Back Door to Success.*) Hallelujah! What a fantastic book. I haven't even read it; just the title touches my heart!

Fourthly, is Jesus Christ Lord over your resources?

That perhaps is the toughest issue. Materialism doesn't go out easily. We have trouble even acknowledging it. It's always the other guy that's more materialistic than us. AW Tozer said that 'materialism will not go out easily by raising your hand. It will go out like a tooth being extracted from the jaw.'

My dear brothers and sisters, if we don't deal with materialism in the church and in our own lives and put our resources on the altar and use it as God would have us use it, then I don't believe we will reach these unreached people.

Honesty

I give a plea for honesty and integrity in our publicity, in describing what we do, in our conversations with one another. Let's not pretend we're living up here if we know we're living down here. Let's get in honest fellowship with one another and share and confess our faults one with another as the Word of God teaches.

Reality

Reality with God. Knowing God must be our first priority, even more important than world missions. Read some of those great books by men like Tozer and Andrew Murray and JI Packer and others.

Purity

We've already touched on this as we've talked about Christ being Lord over our social and emotional life. Often when we talk about purity, we are reminded of David. Praise God for the forgiveness we see in David. It needs to be emphasized. I believe in it, but for young people I've got something more exciting than David. Those of you who are just beginning your life: Joseph! That's the guy that challenges me, because I want to stick as close as I can to Plan A.

Plan A means that you live a life of purity before God and before men from the moment of your conversion. Joseph was tempted with this voluptuous beauty – can you imagine it? I don't even like to imagine it. This chick – whooo! – kept offering herself to Joseph. You know he's lonely; he's a man. But he said, 'I will not do this wicked thing,' and he wins the victory.

We always think when you win a victory like that you get a reward, right? You get a lovely Christian girlfriend the next day. No, he got prison. Prison! And that was before co-education.

Discipline

Without it and the message of 1 Corinthians 9 where Paul says, 'I buffet my body and bring it into subjection,' we're not going to go very far. The way ahead is going to be rough and tough.

Vision

Let's pray, as we close in prayer now, that God would increase our vision for the whole world – for the fields that are ripe unto harvest.

And finally, my favourite word: *Action*

If you believed this roof was going to fall in, what would you do? Write a little chorus about falling roofs? Have a theological discussion about falling roofs? No, if you believed this roof was going to fall in you would move. You would mobilize.

Last night, a terrible fire broke out at this time in Champaign[2] and destroyed a complete city block. Let's pray for the people who were involved. I don't think anyone is seriously hurt. If we believed right now that a fire was starting underneath this building (as we had underneath the escalator system in London in the subway recently that destroyed so many people) what would we do? We would move.

Brothers and sisters, the world is on fire. The harvest is plenteous, the labourers are few. Satan is trying to hinder at every turn. Let us rise up. Let us mobilize and let us go forth making Jesus Christ absolute Lord every day of our life until we are with him. Amen.

---

[1] This message was given at InterVarsity Christian Fellowship's "Urbana '87" convention at the University of Illinois in December 1987. The spoken text has been slightly edited for readability. Copyright InterVarsity Christian Fellowship. Used by permission.

[2] Champaign is the city adjoining Urbana, where this message was preached.

Section 1

Personal Reformation, Reality and Revival

Finance seems to be the greatest obstacle...The real obstacle is a lack of love, faith and biblical commitment. We can't separate what I'm saying here from personal reformation, reality and revival. It is a mistake to think that the next big move is God's. His big moves have already taken place. The Cross; the empty tomb; and Pentecost. **NOW IT IS OUR TURN!!** We need to repent and turn from all that is hindering us from doing God's will in our day.

George Verwer[1]

---

[1] Unless noted, section and chapter introductory quotations were downloaded from {www.georgeverwer.com} in October 2002.

Keeping On for the Long Haul

Grace Ferguson

... it all comes down to the discipline of daring, of being willing to take risks for God. This is what the life of faith is, by definition... We must be willing as Caleb to dare, to gamble and trust.

George Verwer

Some years ago a leader from another mission visited us with a lengthy questionnaire designed to help their incoming team adjust. One question he asked was, 'What has been the hardest thing for you about living on the mission field?' My answer, neither expected nor understood, was simply, 'Staying.' Later on their team did come, but they didn't stay.

The devil tries desperately to keep Christians from entering missions. If you do go, he may try to make you miserable, scare you away, wear you out and discourage you. Fellow missionaries or mission leaders may cause the most pain. If you don't give up and leave, the enemy will try to make you ineffective and upset. Since we claim Christ as Lord, we accept the testing and trials he allows as his best plan to accomplish his will in the country where he has brought us. When you encounter trouble, don't turn back, but keep going with God's help.

In 1970 we graduated from college. Within three months we married and moved to the Middle East. With God's help, we have tried to 'run with perseverance the race marked out for us' (Heb. 12:1). God has given us what we needed for each day.

Sunday: The Lord's Day for Worship

Our primary calling is to 'Worship the Lord your God and serve him only' (Matt. 4:10). Only Jesus is worthy of the cost you will pay to persevere. Check your motivation as you set out and be sure that you are not going into missions to please a leader, a team, a mission, a church, a friend or parents. Any sacrifice you make should be for Christ's sake alone. If Christ has called you, follow him in loving obedience that will take precedence over any other attachment, dream, thought or comfort.

One of our main sources of encouragement is fellowship with the local body of Christ. We must persevere in our ability to read the Bible and pray in a new language, in our adaptation to new conditions, in our waiting to be accepted and included and in our patience with their differences. The way to keep going is to get the focus correct and keep our priorities straight.

Monday: Washing with Humility

All of the Middle East is dusty, and living in a city of six million adds grime to the dust, so clothes need to be washed frequently. When our boys were small my husband came home with a copy of Edith Schaeffer's book *Hidden Art* as a present for me. Every few days I had to boil up a huge pot of cloth diapers on the stove, rinse them out in the bathtub and carefully hang them out to dry over the front of our balcony on the fourth floor, hoping they wouldn't drop and that they would dry before it rained or there was a dust storm. My only opportunity for hidden art seemed to be how I hung the diapers! And I had to keep washing them.

Similarly, without regular spiritual cleansing, we will not be able to go for the long haul because of sin in our lives and broken relationships with others. In our ministry we have spent a lot of time cleaning up relations or situations for spiritual babies. We must humbly do whatever is necessary to wash away entanglements and sin in our lives and others'.

Tuesday: Food Shopping with Contentment

Many of my hours as a missionary homemaker have been spent buying, preparing, cooking, and serving food. I was encouraged one day by Matthew 24:45 NIV, 'Who then is the faithful and wise servant, whom the master has put in charge of the servants in his household to give them their food at the proper time?' God notices when we faithfully feed the children He gives us and the guests He sends. The test is to be content both with the food we have to eat and the work we need to do to have it. You won't stay long on the mission field if you continually yearn for and try to eat or have what you had at 'home'. Keep trying, tasting, and learning how to prepare and eat local food. If you don't like something the first time, maybe you will by the twentieth!

Hospitality is very important in the Middle East. Honour is shown to guests by preparing the best food you can in more than ample amounts. Eating together provides opportunity for fellowship and informal teaching of new believers. When we share the gospel, we must also share our lives.)

We have experienced God's supernatural provision in times of need and crisis. When the civil war broke out in Lebanon, our Palestinian doorman would warn us not to go out on the days the fighting was too fierce, telling us, 'Stay home today and I will bring you bread.' In our early years of ministry, we experienced shortages of many food staples. Each time, local believers would bring us what we needed, although we had not told them of our need.

Contentment has even more to do with the nourishment of our spirits. If we do not know how to feed ourselves spiritually by reading, studying and meditating on the Word of God, we will not make it for the long haul. There may be no Sunday school classes, conferences, marriage enrichment weekends, Christian camps, Christian radio and TV or even a church where God calls you to serve. But God can provide all we need for life and godliness.

Wednesday: Working with Faithfulness

We are set apart for the work which God has called us to do, but our job description may change many times. Our first task is to learn the language and become as much as possible like the people we serve. Success in learning a language is directly proportional to the time spent, and a fundamental motivator is our love for the people. Without love, we will not accomplish anything of lasting spiritual value. Later we can use our spiritual gifts cross-culturally in evangelism, teaching, tent making, office work, preaching, producing literature, films or music.

The motives of our heart are revealed by our reactions. Are we working to bring glory to Christ or to ourselves? After working several years in one city doing door-to-door evangelism and faithfully participating in all the activities of the local church, we were asked not to attend a special meeting for correspondence course students from a radio ministry. I wept when we were not included, but I learned an important lesson. It is God's work, not ours. Ultimately, the evangelism of any country is the responsibility of the people of that country and our role is to faithfully encourage and support them.

We are servants of Jesus Christ and he is the one who assigns each servant his task and the time, place and duration of his work. Everyone is given a different task and that is why we are commanded not to judge and not to compare ourselves with one another. We are admonished, 'Whatever you do, work at it with all your heart, as working for the Lord, not for men' (Col. 3:23 NIV).

Thursday: Travelling with Thankfulness

One thing is guaranteed if you make it for the long haul; you will become an expert at packing and unpacking suitcases! Your first goodbyes will probably be to parents and siblings with little understanding of the sacrifices both you and they will make in the years to come. Later on it will be goodbyes to grown up children. Your commitment to 'leave family and home for Christ's sake' (Matt. 19:29) will have to be remade over and over. Separation never gets easier.

Each return visit to your home country may bring a different battle. Friends will have houses, jobs, possessions and security that you will never have. Relatives may not understand why you don't quit, come home, settle down and get a *real* job. The devil will subtly suggest, 'Look what you could have, if you stayed home.' One cost of leaving your passport culture and adjusting to another culture is that you no longer completely fit or belong in your home country.

Being set apart for the work of the Gospel, our lifestyle is different. One day our oldest son phoned from college and encouraged us to keep on living by faith. He understood that our life is like that of the Levites who were given no inheritance or share in the land because God was their share and inheritance (Num. 18:20). We need to guard our hearts from jealousy, grumbling, discontent, and striving for something that God hasn't provided. Filling our hearts with thankfulness will keep the other things out!

Friday: Payday for Perseverance

In our tenth year of ministry, I became discouraged by the lack of visible fruit. Why were so few coming to faith? Why were the new believers not going on? Through the parable of the sower, God reminded me that our responsibility was to sow the seed even if the soil where we were working was rocky, hard and dry. On judgment day, God would be declared just because of our obedience to proclaim His message of salvation to a group of people who would be judged according to their response to that message. We needed to focus on what God had sent us to do. 'You must go to everyone I send you to and say whatever I command you' (Jer. 1:7 NIV).

If we choose to accept God's call, we will face pain, suffering, loss and testing. Jesus learned obedience from what He suffered and likewise, God will not spare any lesson, testing, or trial that we need to teach us obedience. (If it had been up to us, we might not have chosen the experiences that God brought into our lives.)

During our first year of language study we travelled to another country at Christmas to do gospel distribution. In an obscure town with no church, we were arrested, questioned and blacklisted so that we could not get permanent residence in that country.

Because of summer evangelism in a closed country, my husband spent eight and a half months of our second year of marriage in prison with three others. I went through my first pregnancy and delivery alone. Although they were sentenced to four years in prison, God released them thirteen days after our first son was born.

During a ceasefire in the Lebanese civil war, my husband decided to go back with three others and bring our things to Jordan. Their vans were stopped at gunpoint just as they left Tripoli, Lebanon, heading south on the coastal road to Beirut. Armed militia ordered them to drive into some orange groves and get out of the vans. The armed men drove away with the vans and everything in them, but no lives were lost.

The summer of 1989 we arranged for a large group of Arab believers to participate in summer evangelism in Europe. We planned a family vacation in Cyprus after my husband's return and before the school year began. It was a wonderful week camping and hiking in the mountains and swimming at the beach. The day after we returned home, our third son went to visit a friend. A few hours later his friend phoned. Our son had been killed in a skateboard accident.

Suffering has given us a heart link with Middle Eastern believers who suffer for their faith. To persevere we have had to endure persecutions and trials. Our perseverance comes from a commitment of love.

'Therefore, my dear brothers, stand firm. Let nothing move you. Always give yourselves fully to the work of the Lord because you know that your labor in the Lord is not in vain' (1 Cor. 15:58 NIV).

Saturday: A Day Off for Rest

Going for the long haul is like running a marathon. We need to pace ourselves, count the cost and think about future results of current decisions. There will be different phases in our lives and ministry with different strengths and limitations. Without a healthy balance of work and rest, we would have been unable to keep going.

We have wonderful memories of family days, vacations, exploring the countries where we have lived, picnics, cook outs, days at the beach, visits with relatives, trips to the park and the zoo, conferences, and retreats. Getting away has refreshed us, renewed us and enabled us to go back, pick up the plow and faithfully work the ground where God has placed us.

My first year in the Middle East, I was privileged to live with a Jordanian family. They had a tiny bathroom where we took showers by heating a tub of water and pouring it over ourselves with a large plastic cup. Since the Palestinian pastor and his wife in that town had a bathtub, they insisted that my Swedish teammate and I come to their home every week to take a bath! Those baths, followed by plates of fruit, cake and tea were God's provision for rest and change.

After we have persevered and done the will of God, we will rest from our work and share in Jesus' joy. We will worship him in his beauty and rejoice in his love. All the stains from our sins and others will be removed by his purity. Any lack of contentment, faithfulness or thanksgiving will be forgiven. Any suffering will be a humble offering to One so glorious.

'Therefore, since through God's mercy we have this ministry, we do not lose heart' (2 Cor. 4:1 NIV)

During the years of our long haul, God has touched many hearts to provide our needs. Without them we would probably have been unable to go on. These beatitudes are written for them with our thanks.

Blessed are those who remember us even though we have spent most of our lives away.

Blessed are those who realized we were hungry or tired or needed a vacation and provided what we needed.

Blessed are those who invited us for meals furlough after furlough even though we could never reciprocate.

Blessed are those who remembered us on our birthdays and other holidays.

Blessed are those who supported us financially month after month, year after year.

Blessed are those who loaned us their cars and their homes.

Blessed are those who bought us suits, dresses, shoes and clothes for the children.

Blessed are those who showered us with linens, towels, household equipment, toiletries and stationery.

Blessed are those who gave us medical and dental care free of charge.

Blessed are those who bought us computers and helped us keep abreast of current technology.

Blessed are those who took our children into their homes as if they were their own, gave them work or bought them airplane tickets!

Blessed are those who prayed for us every day.

Blessed are all those who were our fellow labourers in the Gospel.

Grace Ferguson (pseudonym) and her husband have worked with Operation Mobilisation in the Middle East region for over thirty years.

Holiness And Community

Ajith Fernando

We need a constant work of the Holy Spirit. I often tell the story about D.L. Moody who would emphasize the need to be filled with the Spirit again and again. One day when asked, 'Mr. Moody why do you keep saying we have to be filled again and again?' he replied, 'Because I leak'. **Thank God for free refills.**

George Verwer

Holiness, commonly understood in evangelical circles as 'Christ-likeness', is a very important theme in the New Testament. In a statistical study done on the Epistles of Paul, I found that 1400 of the 2005 verses in the Epistles, that is, about 70 per cent of the verses, are in some way connected with the call to be holy. This suggests that it should be an important theme in the teaching of the church today. In this article I hope to focus on the important place that the Bible gives to the part the Christian community plays in Christians becoming holy. I will call this process 'mutual up-building'.

Mutual Up-building

Much of the teaching relating to holiness in the New Testament is given in the plural, implying that growth in holiness takes place within the context of the body. A good example is 1 Corinthians

3:16-17: 'Do you not know that you are God's temple and that God's Spirit dwells in you? If anyone destroys God's temple, God will destroy him. For God's temple is holy, and you are that temple.'[1] The 'you' here is plural.

In my study of Paul's epistles I found several sub-themes that could be classified under the theme of mutual up-building. This is presented in the list below. I have generally left out statements that speak of up-building through the ministry of leaders, and primarily used the texts that indicate that ordinary Christians can help each other grow in holiness:

Our behaviour should aim at mutual up-building; Christian growth takes place in the context of the body: 26 verses[2]

We are to admonish and teach each other: 8 verses[3]

Gifts have been given to be used for mutual up-building: 2 verses[4]

Prophecy is preferred to tongues because it builds others up: 17 verses[5]

Corporate worship is a means God uses to help Christians grow: 4 verses[6]

Christians are to help restore other Christians caught up in sin: 4 verses[7]

Christians grow through observing the examples of other Christians: 30 verses.[8] I included Paul's example, though I have left out long passages like 1 Corinthians 9 where he describes the sacrifices he made for the gospel as an example to follow. This impressive list implies that reading biographies could be a great means of growth for the Christian.

When deciding on a course of action, we are sensitive to the possibility that other Christians may stumble because of things that we consider acceptable: 30 verses.[9]

When I was a theological student I spoke on 2 Timothy 2:22 for my practical test in preaching. It says, 'So flee youthful passions and pursue righteousness, faith, love, and peace, along with those who call on the Lord from a pure heart.' I spoke about the need to flee youthful passions and pursue the virtuous qualities Paul mentioned. After the sermon my preaching professor remarked that I had not dealt with what is possibly the most important point in this verse: that we do the fleeing and the pursuing 'along with those who call on the Lord from a pure heart'.

By this omission I was reflecting the typical evangelical distortion of Christian holiness by turning it into an individualistic rather than a corporate matter. God intends for us to battle for holiness along with fellow Christians. The Protestant Reformation rightly reacted against the Roman Catholic doctrine of salvation through the church by returning to the biblical emphasis on individual salvation. Evangelical movements helped keep this in the forefront when it was later neglected within Protestant churches. But we must not forget that the Bible also teaches that Christians live and grow in community. We need 'a move away from the … emphasis on the individual making up the church, and a move towards an understanding of the church as a formative phenomenon which acts on the life of the believer.'[10]

The way Christians help each other grow in holiness is well expressed in Hebrews 10:25: 'And let us consider how to stir up one another to love and good works, not neglecting to meet together, as is the habit of some, but encouraging one another.' Let me give one example how this verse works. Here is a Christian worker who, after straying a few times into some unclean sites on the Internet, finds that he is strongly compelled to go to pornographic sites. Thousands of Christian workers are struggling with this problem today. But this worker has a group he is accountable to. He shares his problem with the group and they set several guidelines for him including that he regularly reports to the group about his activity in this area. Now, whenever he is tempted to stray, he remembers that he has to report everything to his group. He knows that he may have to face disciplinary action over his failings. There is a check in his spirit that pulls him away from the path of temptation. The pathway is open for him to free himself from the stranglehold of pornography. The process of mutual up-building is described in much detail in Proverbs which has some rich statements on how friends help each other to live godly lives (e.g. Prov. 12:1, 15; 17:10; 19:27; 27:6).[11]

No Theology of Groaning[12]

I often speak in Sri Lanka on the need for Christian workers to have friends who can help them to grow spiritually and with whom they could share their struggles. Many have responded saying that they will not share their problems with other Christians because they have tried before and were deeply hurt. The growing church in Sri Lanka may have a theological problem that hinders Christian workers from sharing problems with friends. We may be concentrating so much on growth, praise and power in church life that we are presenting a Christianity that has no place for the biblical concept of groaning. When people groan about their weaknesses, others often respond wrongly, perhaps rejecting the groaner or telling others what was shared with them in confidence.

I have taken the term *groaning* from Romans 8:23, which says, 'we ourselves, who have the first fruits of the Spirit, groan inwardly as we wait eagerly for adoption as sons, the redemption of our bodies'. Earlier Paul said, 'the creation was subjected to futility' as a result of the Fall (8:20). We do not get everything we want nor do we experience the fullness of perfection that God intends to give us in heaven. But we have a foretaste of it, for we 'have the first fruits of the Spirit' (8:23). We groan because of the disparity between what we will have in heaven and what we have now. Among the things we groan about is our struggle to live a holy life.

A good example of groaning is the lament of the Old Testament. The book of Psalms has fifty to sixty Psalms in which the psalmists complain to God about struggles. If the Holy Spirit inspired so many laments to be recorded in the Bible, then groaning must surely be part of the Christian life. Those who have a theology of lament will have a place for emphasizing honest expressions of struggle which can exist alongside an emphasis on growth, power and praise.

Sometimes we are so eager for growth that we become like advertisers who give only the positive side of a product and avoid talking about the unpleasant sides. Nowadays advertisers are required to mention negative aspects about their product. They usually do so as inconspicuously as possible. Many churches have not caught on to this practice yet! They know that people will be attracted to the church if the message presented shows all the wonderful things that God can do. Problems that Christians face are neglected for marketing reasons. This has happened for so long that many people do not have a place for groaning in their understanding of the Christian life.

When a Christian talks about his or her problems in this environment, other Christians don't know what to do. Those who share could face rejection and public blame for not being good Christians. Therefore they learn to live without talking about their problems, unless it is the type of problem that could become a 'prayer concern'. They will ask for prayer for healing and guidance and provision of a job or funds, but not for overcoming a hot temper or a bad habit or discouragement.

In a sense this is a defective understanding of grace. The biblical understanding of grace is so great that Christians do not need to fear facing up to their sin. Sin is never justified in the Bible and must always be condemned. Grace is greater than sin but grace cannot be applied unless we admit that we have sinned. Therefore, if we desire the fullness of God's grace in our lives, we will be eager to confess our sin so as to open the door to a rich experience of grace. This is not done in a flippant or light way; we are grieved by sin. But we are so eager for cleansing that we will eagerly face up to the sin and seek forgiveness.

1 John 1:5 – 2:3 presents this paradox powerfully. John says, 'My little children, I am writing these things to you so that you may not sin' (1 John 2:1$_a$) – sin is never condoned – 'But if anyone does sin, we have an advocate with the Father, Jesus Christ the righteous. He is the propitiation for our sins' (1 John 2:1$_b$-2). God's grace in Christ is so great that we do not need to fear to face up to sin. In fact we fear not facing up to it for we know that 'if we walk in the light, as he is in the light, we have fellowship with one another, and the blood of Jesus his Son cleanses us from all sin' (1 John 1:7). We dread the prospect of forfeiting the fellowship and the cleansing by not walking in the light. So we will be eager to 'confess our sins' (1 John 1:9).

Defective theologies of groaning and grace can combine to produce a church where people are afraid to express their deep hurts and struggles to other Christians. When a leader has a problem like a deteriorating marriage or bondage to a harmful habit, he may have no one to talk to about it. He valiantly tries to overcome the problem through confession to God, prayer and making firm personal resolutions. But he is caught in a downward spiral, and there seems to be no way out. Finally the problem becomes public, and there is a terrible scandal. This could have been avoided if others had come in and helped this leader out of his mess.

New Testament Community: Life in the Raw

We learn a lot about community life from the description in the Gospels of the life of Jesus and his disciples. There we find what I am calling 'life in the raw'. There is no hiding of the problems of the disciples. Not only did the disciples face up to the problems, the Holy Spirit also saw it fit to have these problems recorded in Scripture so that we could learn something from them. The New Testament writers were not afraid to acknowledge the weaknesses of the first disciples who, at the time of writing, were the key leaders of the church.

Jesus is the only one in the Bible who is without sin. But the Gospels show even Jesus struggling at times. We see him weeping at the funeral of Lazarus (John 11:35). The Gospels do not hide the fact that Jesus really struggled with the will of God in the garden of Gethsemane. Luke describes his struggle thus: 'And being in an agony he prayed more earnestly; and his sweat became like great drops of blood falling down to the ground' (Luke 22:44; see also Matt. 26:37; Mark 14:33). He was in agony because he was finding the will of God for him (bearing the sin of the world on a cross) so difficult to accept. He prays, 'Father, if you are willing, remove this cup from me. Nevertheless, not my will, but yours, be done' (Luke 22:42; see also John 12:27). Strengthened by the results of this struggle, Jesus marches so triumphantly to the cross that those who came to arrest him 'drew back and fell to the ground' when he introduced himself to them (John 18:6)!

We often wish to avoid something that we know we should do, and Jesus' frank confession of his feelings to God gives us the courage to express our apprehensions. When we do so, others in the community should not judge us but sympathize and help give us the courage to be obedient. Our expression of need provides the trigger for God's work of strengthening us for tough challenges.

The important thing is to be obedient. Those who never express their fears sometimes end up disobeying God. They have not really grappled with the problem and are not prepared when it comes, nor do they have anyone to encourage them at their time of need.

A healthy Christian community encourages its members to be open about faults and fears. Their desire for all of God, and their belief in the sufficiency of grace will urge them to confront sin and problems fearlessly and to look for God to use that to purify, teach and deepen the community. A community that deals with problems openly and biblically will become a community with a deep spirituality because God is able to minister and teach his deep truths through the grappling that takes place to solve the problem. This is what happened out of the blunders of the disciples recorded in the Gospels. Each one produced some deep teaching by Christ which made facing up to it so worthwhile.

John Wesley's Bands

Something like the group known as the 'band' which John Wesley advocated among the Methodists can be a great help in the growth in holiness of a Christian. A band was the equivalent of what we today call an accountability group. It is different from Wesley's more popular 'class meeting' which was equivalent to a cell or house group. The class meeting was a heterogeneous group of people living in the same area who met to apply the Scriptures to daily life. Bands were homogeneous groups divided according to sex, age and marital status. Such restrictions encouraged the members to share private things about their personal lives. Wesley's *Rules of the Bands* states: 'The design of our meeting is to obey that command of God, "Confess your faults one to another, and pray for one another that ye may be healed"' (James 5:16). Here Wesley listed six things that they intended to do at this meeting. Two are of special interest to us:

4. To speak to each of us in order, freely and plainly, the true state of our souls, with the faults we have committed in thought, word and

deed, and the temptations we have felt since our last meeting.

6. To desire some person among us to speak his own state first, and then to ask the rest in order, as many and as searching questions as may be, concerning their state, sins, and temptations.[13]

Today many Christian leaders have as their *accountability group* people that they do not work closely with. While 'something is better than nothing' perhaps this is not ideal to help us along the path to holiness. These people do not see us at work and must depend on our reporting to know our situation. Given the inclination of the human heart to deception, it is possible for us to give an inaccurate picture of what is really going on in our lives. For this reason it may be better for us to have an accountability group of people with whom we live and or work closely, such as members of the same church, organization or ministry team.

Given the huge problem with unholiness in today's church, we should be giving more stress on the place that the Christian community has in helping Christians to become holy. I am delighted by the privilege of writing on this topic for a book published in honour of George Verwer. Through the honesty that characterizes his proclamation and writing he has given the church a very helpful example of 'life in the raw' and brought holiness down to a level that is practically applicable to fellow pilgrims like me![14]

Ajith Fernando has been Director of Youth for Christ in Sri Lanka since 1976. He and his wife Nelun are also active in a local Methodist Church most of whose members are from Buddhist backgrounds. Ajith also has a Bible teaching ministry at seminaries and conferences in Sri Lanka and abroad. He has written eleven books. Ajith and Nelun reside in Colombo with their son and daughter.

---

[1] The Bible version used in this article is the *English Standard Version* (Wheaton: Crossway Bibles, 2001).

[2] Rom. 14:19; 15:1-2; 1 Cor. 3:10; 8:1; 10:24, 33; 12:7-27; Eph. 4:29; 6:21-22; 1 Thess. 3:2; 5:11, 14; 1 Tim. 4:16; 2 Tim. 2:22

3   Rom. 15:14; Eph. 4:15; Col. 3:16; 4:17; 1 Thess. 4:18; 5:14; 2 Thess. 3:15; 2 Tim. 2:2

4   1 Cor. 12:7; 14:12

5   1 Cor. 14:1-12, 18-19, 29-31

6   1 Cor. 10:16-17; 14:26; Col. 3:16

7   Gal. 6:1-2; 2 Thess. 3:14-15

8   1 Cor. 4:16-17; 11:1; 2 Cor. 1:12; 4:2; 6:4-10; 7:2; 11:23, 27; Gal. 4:12; Phil. 3:17; 1 Thess. 1:5-7; 2:14; 5:12-13; 2 Thess. 3:7-9; Tit. 2:7-8; 2 Tim. 3:10-11

9   Rom. 14:1-7, 13-23; 1 Cor. 8:7-13; 1 Cor. 10:28-29, 32-33; 2 Cor. 6:3

10 From a review by Sean O'Callaghan of Simon Chan, *Pentecostal Theology and the Christian Tradition* (Sheffield: Sheffield Academic Press, 2000) in *Themelios* 27:1, Autumn 2001, 87.

11 The many statements in Proverbs about how we can help each other grow in holiness provided the base for a book I wrote entitled, *Reclaiming Friendship* (Leicester: InterVarsity Press, 1991 and Harrisburg, PA: Herald Press, 1994).

12 An expanded version of what is given below appears in my book, *Jesus Driven Ministry* (Wheaton: Crossway Books, 2002), chapter 9: 'Growing in a Team'

13 D. Michael Henderson, *John Wesley's Class Meeting: A Model for Making Disciples* (Nappance, IN: Evangel Publishing House, 1997), 117-18.

14 I was particularly helped by his books *No Turning Back* and *Out of the Comfort Zone*.

Worship and Mission

Frank Fortunato

Whenever I want an intimate time with the Lord I put on my praise tapes. The louder and faster the better. This helps me worship.

George Verwer[1]

The *fuel* of worship is a true vision of the greatness of God;
the *fire* that makes the fuel burn white-hot is the quickening of the Holy Spirit;
the *furnace* made alive and warm by the flame of truth is our renewed spirit;
the resulting heat of our affections is powerful worship.

John Piper[2]

It stunned me. My spiritual radar had been more or less on stand-by. I sensed God say something like: 'Frank! Get this. I've been waiting for you to come to this moment in your life.'

That moment was an insight into worship. A horrible auto accident on a trip home from Asia to Europe had set the stage for this encounter with the Lord. Four fellow workers with Operation Mobilisation died in an auto crash, including the young lady I was about to marry. One of two survivors, I had been in a coma with broken bones from skull to big toe. I had lost most of my vision over several days of unconsciousness. My corneas blistered from exposure due to eyelids that did not close properly. The exposure left scarring in both eyes.

Several eye surgeries later, a portion of vision began to return. I had a voracious desire to read after weeks in hospital. I grabbed the first thing I spotted, a tiny anthology of Tozer quotes. The words of the inside cover chiseled their way into my being: 'The Christian conception of God…is so decadent as to be utterly beneath the dignity of the Most High…With our loss of the sense of majesty has come the further loss of religious awe and consciousness of the divine Presence.'[3]

Quote after quote from that little anthology went through me like a surgical knife. While American surgeons had worked hard to salvage physical vision, the Divine Surgeon went deep into my soul to clarify spiritual vision. Different shafts of light kept penetrating me with thoughts like: 'You've been a musician for me, Frank. But that's not enough! I allowed you to survive the accident because you have a higher calling. Learn to worship!' My adventure of a lifetime began that very moment.

Richard Foster wrote 'Worship…is not for the timid or comfortable. It involves an opening of ourselves to the adventurous life of the Spirit.'[4] This brief essay reflects on some of the principles and practices gathered from the journey.

1. Principles

It's all about him

Worship is the most important ministry for the Christian – the one activity that will continue into eternity. The truly radiant people of the earth are those most enraptured by the Lord. Worship leader and author Vivien Hibbert describes one such person who played a humble role in a church orchestra in South America:

> The little lady was stuck behind the piano, scarcely able to see or be seen. She played a pair of finger cymbals. Despite the fact that she was never heard by anyone except God, she stayed poised for action, eyes ablaze with expectancy from the first note of the first song, right through to the last note of the conference. She gave her all and played her part with great diligence and devotion. Many musicians would have clamored for visibility or a microphone before they would have

consented to play during worship. This woman, however, was only interested in pleasing the Lord through her worship as she counted it an honor to play with the other musicians. She was clearly ministering to God with all her heart, mind, and strength ... My life was changed as I worshiped with her.[5]

Despite the global phenomenon of the growth of worship, too often devotion is swallowed up in debate and emotion over stylistic preferences. As worship author and songwriter Gerrit Gustafson has said, 'How quickly our preferences become biases. And how easily our biases become walls that keep us from the larger Body of Christ and from fuller expressions of worship'. That's what makes Matt Redman's modern classic song so poignant: 'I'm coming back to the heart of worship, and it's all about You' – a song which grew out of a controversial season in his church.

The beginning and the end of worship is the Alpha and Omega himself, the Lord of the Universe, an Awesome God worthy of our total devotion and adoration. He has always been and will always be. The great Omnipotent, Omnipresent, Omniscient I AM who I AM, is worthy! In worship, (literally 'worth-ship') we declare his worthiness.

I read about an elderly Christian woman who declared his worthiness to the very end. As she began to lose her memory she could recite just one verse from the New Testament. Even that one verse starting slipping from memory until in her final days all she could remember was: 'Him, Him, Him!' She had lost the whole Bible, except for that one powerful word. But yet she *had* the whole Bible in that one word: Him!

Attributes and actions

Preoccupation with him centers upon his character, ways, attributes and actions. Who could not possibly bow in astonished wonder and worship encountering a verse like Psalm 147:4 'he determines (counts, appoints) the number of stars and calls them each by name'. God spoke the hundreds of billions of galaxies into existence. One British scientist proclaimed there are more stars in the universe than the total number of sand crystals covering the shores of planet Earth. And God has each star named! Time to burst into the old hymn: 'I see the stars...Thy power throughout the universe displayed. Then sings my soul, my Saviour, God, to Thee, How great Thou art!'

Many believe the attributes and acts of God revealed in the word are by no means exhaustive. There will be an ongoing uncovering of who God is throughout eternity. When John in the spirit stood before the Throne (Rev. 4; 5) he saw the elders and living creatures continuously falling before the Lord. What probably triggered the continuous falling was new revelation about the Lord that came, over and over again. As Hibbert reminds us: 'there is not enough time in all eternity to complete the uncovering...of God's character. The depths of the knowledge of God are everlasting.'[6]

Meditation leading to worship

Contemplating the attributes and actions of our Almighty God involves the process of meditation. In J.I. Packer's classic book *Knowing God* he challenges us:

> How can we turn our knowledge about God into knowledge of God? The rule for doing this is demanding but simple. It is that we turn each truth that we learn about God into a matter for meditation before God, leading to prayer and praise to God...Whatever God is He is completely and simultaneously in all of each attribute, all the time. God's character and attributes are infinitely limitless...Nothing will so enlarge the intellect, nothing so magnify the whole soul of man, as a devout, earnest, continued investigation of the great subject of God...So plunge yourself in the Godhead's deepest sea; be lost in its immensity; and you shall come forth refreshed and invigorated.[7]

Charles Spurgeon adds: 'Let your soul lose itself in holy wonder, which will lead you to grateful worship.'[8]

Worship and Word

We don't gather to share our own concoctions of who God is, but to discover what God has chosen to reveal about Himself through the word. John Stott put it this way: 'God must speak to us before we have any liberty to speak to him. He must disclose to us who he is before we can offer him what we are in acceptable worship. The worship of God is always a response to the Word of God. Scripture wonderfully directs and enriches our worship.'[9]

Missionary and worship speaker Ron Man adds: 'In order for worship to be filled with the wonder of God, that wonder must be displayed through the reading and exposition of the mighty acts and ways of God as related to us in Scripture. That's why John Piper refers to preaching as "expository exultation".'[10]

Transformation

No scripture has captured my imagination like 2 Corinthians 3:18 (NASB). 'But we all with unveiled face beholding as in a mirror the glory of the Lord are being *transformed into the same image* from glory to glory, just as by the Spirit of the Lord.' William McDonald referred to this passage as 'changed by beholding'. As we peer into the mirror of God's Word, the Lord allows his own image to be reflected. Paul dares to say we are transformed into that image, incrementally, from glory to glory, by the work of the Spirit in our lives. Breathtaking!

Presence

True worship is connecting with the awesome presence of the Lord. Again Tozer punctures us with his insights: 'The instant cure of most of our religious ills would be to enter the Presence in spiritual experience, to become suddenly aware that we are in God and God is in us. This would lift us out of our pitiful narrowness and cause our hearts to be enlarged. This would burn away the impurities from our lives.'[11]

Over fourteen years serving on the OM ships many memorable moments of God's presence have been carved into my memory. On a church team one Resurrection Sunday in the Caribbean, I went to a Brethren Assembly more preoccupied with the sermon I had to preach than with the Resurrected Lord. I did not expect much from the *a cappella* worship about to begin. No praise bands, synthesizers or sound systems. Just God's people singing their heart out with great abandon. Someone called out the first hymn and the singing began. Full volume, slow, energetic, every word vigorously sung. The power of the Resurrection became so real in the midst of those hymns sung with such vitality. The Spirit of God ignited the Word of God in those lyrics resulting in a divine combustion: worship.

Silence

Most worship discussion rightly deals with biblical responses to God, and Scripture calls us to wholehearted clapping, singing, dancing, shouting, extolling, etc. An often overlooked aspect of corporate worship is silence. 'Be still and know that I am God' (Psa. 46:10). Too often I'm more accustomed to filling in every moment, even playing in the background during intros, transitions, prayers, etc. Andrew Hill tells us: 'The silence of worship is equally as important as the noise of worship…Silence is valuable in Christian worship because it is disturbing, arresting. We feel uncomfortable, helpless; we are no longer in control.'[12] Tozer concurs: 'With our loss of the sense of majesty has come the further loss of religious awe and consciousness of the divine Presence. We have lost our spirit of worship and our ability to withdraw inwardly to meet God in adoring silence.'[13]

II. Practices

Worship and obedience

Worship is never an end in itself unrelated to other aspects of our life. What leads on from congregational worship is lifestyle worship, expressed in loving obedience. Foster states: 'If worship does not propel us into greater obedience, it has not been worship. Holy obedience saves worship from becoming an opiate, an escape from the pressing needs of modern life.'[14] Three key passages for further study are 1 Corinthians 10:31, Colossians 3:17 and Romans 12:1.

Personal devotions

For most, the personal encountering of God relates to the daily 'devotional time', that regular time and place to personally meet with God. Believers worldwide read or pray through hymns as a great source of devotional literature. One motivation for weary joggers like me is the mental and emotional delight that comes from listening to praise tapes while groaning through another set of kilometers!

Worship and evangelism

'Give thanks to the Lord, call on His name; make known His deeds among the peoples. Sing to Him, sing praises to Him; tell of all His wonderful works' (1 Chron. 16:8–9 NRSV). Until we gather eternally at the throne, worship is meant to lead to mission, and praise to proclamation. Urbana worship leader Sundee Frazier reminds us,

> If God is love, how can we leave worship times unmoved by the plight of those who don't know His love? After spending an hour a morning in God's presence, how can we not tell our family, our friends, or future friends, about Jesus? True worship, then, should motivate me to share the love of Jesus just as I have experienced it in worship.[15]

The act of sharing our faith can be worship, as we declare what God had done for us personally through Jesus. Ron Man echoes this:

> To the Apostle Paul, evangelism was in itself an act of worship: 'For God, whom I serve [or worship] in my spirit in the preaching of the gospel of his Son, is my witness…' (Romans 1:9) Paul also considered it to be a spiritual offering of worship for him to present new Gentile converts to God (Romans 15:16).16

Worship and church planting

Music and worship also connect to church planting. Worship musician and missionary Dave Hall created a division of Pioneers

Mission with the purpose of placing a worship musician on every Pioneers church planting team. The dual purpose of the musician was to facilitate times of worship with the church planting team, and then to have a ministry with new believers who were musical to encourage them to develop indigenous worship in emerging churches.

In his book *Tribal Challenge and the Church's Response* former Operation Mobilisation worker S.D. Ponraj relates his experience in Bihar, North India, among various tribal groups. Ponraj purchased local instruments, collected local stories, learned local songs and printed song books. Tribal people loved to sing songs that were a vital part of their culture. The tribal Christians helped Ponraj and his wife learn local songs and apply Christian content. The content of the songs was accepted because the music was good. He printed the songs and gave them to children in the schools; soon the songs were sung everywhere. The use of songs, along with telling of stories and showing of the *Jesus* film, and much follow-up over eight years resulted in thousands turning to the Lord and over 100 congregations established.

Planting worshiping churches will inevitably raise issues of culture. Worship is expressed in culturally determined forms that hopefully reflect biblical principles. But what works in one culture may not necessarily transfer across cultures. While at the Global Consultation on World Evangelization in Pretoria, South Africa, we witnessed a cultural collision in worship. Most African groups present probably used or accepted dance in worship. One such group on the platform danced using warlike gestures as a means of showing their tribal movements redeemed for the Lord. Another African group found those dance movements both offensive and disrespectful. The same form gave totally different meanings. Missiologists continuously remind church planters that our patterns of worship should be seen and accepted as indigenous to each culture.

As worship will be our preoccupation throughout eternity, any brief essay is hardly more than a fleeting snapshot. Dave Hall aptly pulls the threads together with his brilliant *Worship Manifesto* prepared for the AD 2000 Movement Worship and Arts Network[17]:

Worship is both a life to live and an event in which to participate. In and through worship, we, by grace, center our whole being on God, humbly glorifying Him in response to His attributes, His acts and His Word. We covenant together to submit our entire being to God, asking Him to awaken our conscience by His holiness, nourish our mind with His truth, purify our imagination by His beauty, open our heart to His love, and enable us to surrender fully to His purpose. We affirm that unity and cooperation are necessary to complete the task of establishing worshipping communities of Jesus' disciples among every people. Furthermore, we affirm the privilege of each people group to employ all worthy elements of their mother tongue and culture as they worship the Triune God both individually and corporately, in spirit and truth.

Frank Fortunato began ministry with Operation Mobilisation in 1972 serving for many years on the ships Logos *and* Doulos. *Currently Frank is OM's International Music Director, coordinating Heart Sounds International, a ministry of indigenous worship recording projects. Based in Atlanta, Frank also coordinates the International Worship and Arts Network and leads worship at churches and missions-related events. Frank, from the USA, and Berit, from Sweden have two grown children and an adopted child from India.*

[1] George Verwer, personal correspondence with the author, 1996.

[2] John Piper, *Let the Nations Be Glad: The Supremacy of God in Missions.* (Grand Rapids: Baker Books, 1993), p.15

[3] A.W. Tozer, *Gems from Tozer* (Bromley: Send the Light, 1969), p. i

[4] Richard J. Foster, *Celebration of Discipline* (San Francisco: Harper, 1988[rev]), p. 173

[5] Vivien Hibbert, *Prophetic Worship—Releasing the Presence of God* (Dallas: Cuington Press, 1999), p. 222

[6] Hibbert, p. 44

[7] J.I. Packer, *Knowing God* (London: Hodder & Stoughton, 1973), p. 20

[8] Charles H. Spurgeon, *Evening by Evening* (Pittsburgh: Whitaker House, 1984), p. 28

[9] John Stott, *The Contemporary Christian* (Downers Grove: InterVarsity Press, 1992), p. 174

[10] Ron Man, 'God's Global Purpose', {www.firstevan.org/articles.htm}, 2001

[11] A.W. Tozer, *The Pursuit of God* (Camp Hill: Christian Publications, 1993), p. 36

[12] Andrew E. Hill, *Enter His Courts With Praise!* (Grand Rapids: Baker, 1985), p. 102

[13] Tozer, 1969, p. i

[14] Foster, p. 173

[15] Urbana 2000. Worship at Urbana, 2000, downloaded July 7, 2001 from {www.urbana.org/_u2000.cfm}

[16] 'God's Global Purpose', p. 1

[17] {www.worship-arts-network.com/Vision%20statement.html}, downloaded November 19, 2002

Intercession

Juliet Thomas

*My life is full of unanswered prayer. Not even 50 per cent of my prayers have been answered over the years, not yet at least. **I refuse to be discouraged by this**.*
George Verwer

The great cry of our day is work, work, work, organize, organize, organize. Give us some new society, tell us some new methods, devise some new machinery, but the great need of our day is more and better prayer. God wants to speak to us more than we want to listen to Him. Prayer is not therefore begging God to do something He does not want to do. Prayer is simply a heart communion with God – a dialogue between two people who love one another. Prayer arises out of a vital union with God. We do not pray because we have to but because we want to. Time spent with the Lord touches us and enables us to see people and circumstances from the divine perspective.

While preaching on the mighty power of prayer, Spurgeon cried:

The very act of prayer is a blessing. To pray is, as it were, to bathe oneself in a cool stream, and so to escape from the heat of earth's summer sun. To pray is to mount on eagle's wings above the clouds and soar to heaven where God dwells. To pray is to enter the treasure house of God and to enrich oneself out of an inexhaustible storehouse. To pray is to grasp heaven in one's arms, to embrace the deity within one's soul and to feel one's body made a temple of the Holy Ghost. Know this power that is in prayer.[1]

Preparing for Prayer

When we come to worship God and pray, let us confess our sins honestly and openly before God. Pride, jealousy, rivalry, hypocrisy, lying, selfishness, covetousness, anger, bitterness, unforgiveness – all need to be dealt with. We deceive ourselves if we think that we can approach a holy God with unholy hearts and lips. When things go wrong we often tend to blame others, when often self is the problem. We need to learn to pray not 'Lord, change my husband and children' but to pray 'Lord, change me!'

> 'Therefore, if you are offering your gift at the altar and there remember that your brother has something against you, leave your gift there in front of the altar. First go and be reconciled to your brother, then come and offer your gift' (Matt. 5:23–25 NIV).

Very strong words but true. As I look back, I find that bitterness and unforgiveness over deep hurts have often been an area of struggle in my life. But, I have learned that when God commands me to do something He also provides the enabling to do it. I have prayed over and over again 'Lord! Fill my heart with your love and clean me of every dirt of anger, hurt and resentment!'

The wonderful spirit of forgiveness and loving compassion expressed by Gladys Staines for the brutal murderers of her husband Graham and her two young sons has touched the nation of India. This radiant testimony expressing God's love in her has done more to honour and glorify God than all the preaching done in his name over the last decade. Noting the Christian tradition of rejecting hatred and violence even in the face of the worst provocation, an Indian Christian leader said, 'prayer and selfless service are our weapons of protests'.

A Conflict with Evil

In our praying, we are caught up in a tremendous conflict between the two kingdoms of God and Satan. It is an all-encompassing battle with the prince of darkness for those that are his captives. Evangelism then can be defined as rescuing captives from Satan's kingdom.

'[God] has delivered us from the domain of darkness and transferred us to the Kingdom of His Beloved Son' (Col. 1:13 NASB).

'For our struggle is not against flesh and blood, but against the rulers, against the authorities, against the powers of this dark world and against the spiritual forces of evil in the heavenly realms' (Eph. 6:12 NIV).

In this battle we must recognize that 'the weapons of our warfare are not of the flesh, but divinely powerful for the destruction of fortresses (2 Cor. 10:4 NASB). Exodus 17:8-13 describes the war between the Amalekites and Israel. Where was the battle decided? In the valley with Joshua? No, it was decided on the mountain with Moses. Victory in the valley is won by intercession in the mountain: as Moses lifted his hands to God in prayer, Joshua overcomes the Amalekites in the valley below. We could win more battles in the valley if we had more intercessors on the mountain, lifting high the rod of God, the Name of Jesus.

Ronald Dunn, in his book *Don't Just Stand There: Pray Something*, says prayer *is* the warfare.[2] Evangelism then is not the attempt to win the battle; it is the mopping up operation. Prayer releases God's power and assures his protection. Let me tell you a story from India.

My friend Ruby's father-in-law was a high-ranking government officer. Out on inspection of the forest reserves, he decided to spend the night in a government rest house. As he arrived, the caretaker came running out trembling with fear. He stuttered 'Sahib, you cannot stay here. A huge python has entered the living room. I have fastened all the windows and doors.'

Mr. Das carried a rifle with him. He gave it to the caretaker and said: 'There is only one bullet. Take careful aim and shoot the python in the head!' Opening a window slightly, he saw the python coiled around the furniture. With bated breath and nervous fingers that one bullet was shot directly at the python's head. The wounded python reeled and thrashed out. It was dying but in its death throes it destroyed every bit of furniture, crushed and broke the chandeliers, the chairs and everything in that room. After one hour, the python slowly subsided until finally it dropped dead.

Mr. Das added, 'That python is like Satan. Christ has hit that one bullet on Calvary by his death on the Cross. So Satan is furious, violent, destructive – but defeated! He's dying! His end is near. His time is limited! That hour is almost up.'

Jesus is the Victor. Since we belong to him, we no longer strive for victory but act from our position of victory. When I appropriated this wonderful truth in my own life, I entered a new dimension of prayer, praise and intercession.

Passion and Compassion for People

God must give us a burden for people who need to know Jesus. We must learn to travail in prayer for their salvation. The Holy Spirit may lay upon us suddenly a heavy burden to pray for someone or some situation. We need to be obedient and make ourselves available to pray. God is trusting us to pray someone through a dangerous and difficult situation. And we must be faithful to pray right there and then till he lifts that burden and floods our hearts with praise.

In South India, a man is pulling a heavy cart tied to him by ropes. Over his shoulders are thrown heavy weights that pull him down. To his skin are stitched over a hundred lines. His tongue is pulled out and a sharp instrument is pierced through it. Through both his cheeks is thrust another sharp instrument. He pours with sweat as in agony he drags the cart along. His wife and children with weights around their shoulders follow him. Why? To fulfil a vow he had taken for favours received from 'gods'.

Intercession is our heart crying out to God for people who do not know the Name of Jesus and are in bondage and pain. Unless our hearts are wrenched with agony over their agony, we will not know what intercession is.

Developing a Prayer Shield

Pastors, leaders and missionaries must pray and be prayed for. Men and women with high-profile leadership and vast dynamic ministries are falling into the snare of lust, financial mismanagement and greed.

Paul asks congregations and individuals to, 'pray also for me, that whenever I open my mouth, words may be given me so that I will fearlessly make known the mystery of the gospel' (Eph. 6:19 NIV). Every Christian worker and ministry needs a prayer team covering them with intercession.

Tele-evangelist Jimmy Swaggart confessed after his scandal was exposed in 1988 that, 'I did not find the victory I sought therefore, I did not seek the help of my brothers and sisters in the Lord…If I had sought the help of those that loved me, with their added strength, I look back now and know that victory could have been mine.'

Standing in the Gap

So much has been written and spoken about Abraham, 'the friend of God'. The Lord is about to wipe out Sodom and Gomorrah. And then, in one of the most astonishing passages of the Scripture, we hear the Lord say: 'Shall I hide from Abraham what I am about to do?' Why does God take the trouble to explain his actions to an individual in terms he can understand? Abraham was the friend of God, partner of God, with whom he wants to share his plans and concerns.

This raises prayer and intercession to a new level. God is taking counsel with Abraham. No longer are they discussing the important subject of a son of Abraham, but the awful destiny of Sodom. As Abraham in fear and trembling pleaded for the city, it could not only have been the concern for Lot's family that motivated his intensity. It was his wider concerns for other people in Sodom. Surely a just God could not possibly plan to destroy everybody? It is a perplexed man who steps forward to speak, perplexed with the apparent horror of God's judgment.

'Will you sweep away the righteous with the wicked? … Far be it from you! Will not the Judge of all the earth do right?' (Gen. 18:23,25 NIV) His faith was being shattered in a God whom he had hitherto known as just and faithful. He was torn between his terror of God Almighty and his deep yearning to understand that God was just in spite of what he planned to do. The issue here was not the fate of Sodom, but the very character of God.

'Behold, I have ventured to speak to the Lord, although I am *but* dust and ashes' (Gen. 18:25 NASB). Abraham was painfully aware of his creatureliness, his utter insignificance before his creator God. So easily we lose that sense of awe in our worship of God.

Through this terrifying yet wonderful experience of God as he interceded for a doomed city of men and women, Abraham 'grew into a larger man with a greater God. God himself drew the interview to a close and left Abraham to the wonder of his new discovery,' concludes John White.[3] When we touch God in interceding for others, we ourselves experience the deep touch of God in the very depth of our souls.

Intercession, then, is not only bringing our burdens before the throne of grace but is growing in intimacy with God such that God makes us his confidant as we make ourselves available to discern burdens and concerns on his heart.

Keeping a Prayer Watch

History records how the Moravians took up God's concerns upon their own hearts through sustained group praying. This brought forth great revivals. In 1727 the Moravian community of Herrnhut in Saxony commenced a round-the-clock prayer watch that continued for over one hundred years.

On August 27 of that year 24 men and 24 women covenanted to spend one hour each day in scheduled prayer. Soon others enlisted. For over a hundred years the members of the Moravian Church all shared in the hourly intercession. At home and abroad, on land and sea, this prayer watch ascended unceasingly to the Lord,' stated historian A.J. Lewis. By 1792, just 65 years later, the Moravian community had sent out 300 missionaries to the ends of the earth.[4]

That prayer watch was instituted by a community of believers whose average age was probably about thirty. Zinzendorf himself was twenty-seven. The prayer vigil by Zinzendorf and the Moravian community sensitized them to attempt the unheard-of mission to reach others for Christ.

One consequence of that prayer bombardment and evangelization explosion was the conversion of John Wesley. The great evangelist's heart was, in his words, 'strangely warmed', and he came to a personal faith in Christ as he attended a Moravian meeting in London in 1738 – eleven years after the commencement of the prayer watch.

Church historians look to the 18th century and marvel at the Great Awakening in England and America which swept hundreds of thousands into God's Kingdom. John Wesley figured largely in that mighty movement and much attention has centred on him. Is it possible that we have overlooked the place which that round-the-clock prayer watch had in reaching John Wesley and, through him and his associates, in altering the course of history?

One wonders what would flow from a commitment in Operation Mobilisation – and in the church in general – to institute a prayer watch for world evangelization, specifically to reach those, in Zinzendorf's words, 'for whom no one cared'.

For Further Reading

Eveyln Christenson, *What God Does When Women Pray*, (Nashville: World Publishing, 2000)

—, *Battling the Prince of Darkness*, (Illinois:Victor Books, 1990)

Wesley L. Duewel, *Touch the World through Prayer* (Grand Rapids: Zondervan, 1986)

—, *Ablaze For God* (Greenwood, Ind.: OMS International, 1989)

Dick Eastman, *Change the World School of Prayer: A Manual for Leaders*. 1976 National Prayer Forum, Tiruvalla, India.

—, *No Easy Road* (Grand Rapids: Baker, 1985)

—, *The Hour That Changes The World* (Grand Rapids: Baker Book House, 1985)

Robert J. Morgan, *On This Day*, (Nashville: Thomas Nelson Publishers, 1997)

Scott A. Moreau, (ed.), *Spiritual Conflict in Today's Mission*, (Nairobi: Association of Evangelicals of Africa, 2000)

Andrew Murray, *Andrew Murray on Prayer*, (New Kensington: Whitaker House, 1998)

Francis Schaeffer, *True Spirituality* (Bromley, Kent: STL, 1979)

A.W. Tozer, *The Knowledge of the Holy*, (New Delhi: Back to the Bible, 1971)

Juliet Thomas serves under Operation Mobilisation, India, as Director of Arpana Women's Ministries, mobilizing interdenominational prayer networks across India. A member of the Lausanne Committee since 1984, she has been honored as a Life Member and served as chair of its Intercession Working Group from 1990 to 1999. The passion of Juliet's heart is for women, prayer and mission. Her husband Edison is a retired research scientist; they are blessed with two children and four grandchildren.

---

[1] Charles H. Spurgeon, *The Power in Prayer* (New Kensington: Whitaker House, 1996)

[2] Ronald Dunn, *Don't Just Stand There...Pray Something!* (Birminham: Scripture Press, 1992)

[3] John White, *People in Prayer* (InterVarsity Press, Leicester, 1978)

[4] 'The Prayer Meeting that Lasted 100 Years', *Decision*, May 1977

God's Faithfulness

Dale Rhoton

Take ownership in the Great Commission like a stockholder does in a company, and in heaven you'll be a rich spiritual millionaire.

George Verwer

'God's attributes are not isolated traits of His character but facets of His unitary being. They are not things-in-themselves; they are, rather, thoughts by which we think of God, aspects of a perfect whole, names given to whatever we know to be true of the Godhead. To have a correct understanding of the attributes it is necessary that we see them all as one' (A.W. Tozer).

Being perfect in all He is and all He does, God is perfect in faithfulness. The writers of Holy Writ used superlatives in describing God's being and His ways. Isaiah wrote, 'O Lord, you are my God; I will exalt you and praise your name, for in perfect faithfulness you have done marvelous things, things planned long ago' (25:1). The Psalmist worshipped God saying, 'Your love, O Lord, reaches to the heavens, your faithfulness to the skies' (36:5).

We see God's faithfulness in His providing us with security, peace and comfort. We also see His faithfulness in His judgments and His mercy in the midst of suffering. When his city was destroyed before his eyes, Jeremiah bowed and proclaimed, 'Great is your faithfulness' (Lam. 3:24).

Over forty years we have experienced God's faithfulness in Operation Mobilisation. He has been faithful to forgive us innumerable times when we have not exhibited the fruits of the Spirit. He has been faithful to guide us, even when we misunderstood his leading and ran ahead of the light on our path or, perhaps, lagged behind. He has been faithful to use us, even when we strayed.

If God Be For Us...

God's faithfulness covers all of life, including providing financially so that the ministry to which God called us will be accomplished.

The method of fund-raising practiced by OM from its inception has sometimes been termed 'releasing finances through prayer'. The logic of this method is simple: an omnipotent God desires to use his children to bring the Good News to all peoples of the world. If we submit to him, he will guide, protect, and provide.

While we have the responsibility to use our minds when seeking guidance, protection and finances, the burden rests ultimately on the Lord himself. We should let prayer partners know how finances can be donated to the organization. But we aim to be sensitive by not placing inappropriate pressure on our partners to give. George Verwer challenged us repeatedly not to tell prayer partners of certain needs. One of his motives was to be sure that the items prayed for came not out of human sympathy but as a direct answer to prayer.

I can recall several times that George held up his Bible and asked, 'Do you really believe this book?' He found certain teachings overwhelming. For example, the Scriptures clearly teach that salvation is found only in Christ. What happens to those who never hear the Gospel?

Did God really create us so significant that our obedience actually shapes the eternity of another individual, even of many others? George found himself echoing the words of the boy's father in Mark 9: 'I do believe; help me overcome my unbelief!' Could it be that George got it wrong? Did the Bible really teach this? Had he misunderstood? If the passion of missions is something man-made, then better for our mission vision to die a natural death. God forbid that we should spend a lifetime trying to convert the world, only to find out that we were more zealous for missions than God was! As we encountered various barriers in our mission work, we sensed a certain security in letting God either confirm our calling or let the vision die.

During one Christmas vacation in the late 1950s, we needed a van to take our small group with its literature to Mexico. If we had let the need be known, there would have been a fair chance that a number of generous supporters would give out of compassion. So George admonished us to tell no one.

Our evening of prayer followed the usual pattern. We prayed for European and Asian nations by name. We had maps all over the floor. We huddled in small groups on our knees, praying for countries about which we knew very little. Until we had looked at the map, we had had only a vague idea where the nations were located. We prayed for lands where the number of national believers among the majority population was about one in a million. We prayed for the authorities to repent and come to Christ. We prayed for churches to be planted. We prayed for radios to be tuned to Christian programs. We prayed for Bible translators. We prayed that the Lord of the harvest would send forth laborers.

We also talked with our Father about a van to take us to Mexico. We told no one else. A few days later one of the students who had been at the prayer meeting had the joy of leading a man to Christ on the streets of Chicago. They decided to meet together regularly to read the Bible. They would do this until Christmas time, when the student would go away for two weeks.

'Where are you going?' asked the new convert.

'To Mexico. There is a group of us students who are going down to distribute Christian literature and talk to men and women about Christ,' replied the student.

The man hesitated and then asked, 'I have a silly question. I have an old van I don't use. You guys couldn't use it for your trip; could you?'

The van ended up being typical of so many vehicles OM would inherit in the years to come! It was on its last leg. Only an omnipotent God could get it there and back – and He did! Praise the Lord for His faithfulness in giving our team a good mechanic as well.

What if that van had not been given? Who knows? Certainly one answer to prayer or one unanswered prayer does not determine a life's direction; it is the accumulation of answers – the working of God's Spirit in our hearts. It is the irresistible power of the Word of God. It is the testimony of the Christian community throughout the ages. That testimony, we note, is two-fold: it consists of both our own foibles and God's faithfulness.

Even in the matter of choosing board members, George shied away from the wealthy and famous. Again his goal was to avoid arranging things in such a way that even if God did not intervene, the mission could go on. Much better to learn early that God was not in it, than to play church or mission.

In August 1957 George and Walter Borchard embarked on what was to be the first OM outreach. They left New Jersey in a van to drive to Wheaton College where they would pick me up and the three of us would travel on to Mexico. On the first lap of the trip, before reaching Wheaton, the engine gave up. George phoned a close friend for advice, a businessman who had cheered him on in his mission vision and later became one of the original OM board members. He instructed George to put in another engine and continue on. He also arranged to pay for the engine.

How did George's handling of this financial need differ from the ways of professional fund-raisers? I have not asked George that question, but I can hear him saying, 'So much of this is semantics.' He would cringe if someone suggested his way was more spiritual than someone else's method. George was strongly influenced by the life and practice of many individuals and ministries in the 'faith mission' tradition. Notable examples include George Mueller, Hudson Taylor, and William MacDonald.

The prayer promises in the Bible leave no room for doubt. God is eager to hear and answer prayers. He even chides us for not asking more! 'Call to me and I will answer you and tell you great and unsearchable things you do not know' (Jer. 33:3). 'Ask and it will be given to you; seek and you will find; knock and the door will be opened to you' (Matt. 7:7). 'If two of you on earth agree about anything you ask for, it will be done for you by my Father in heaven' (Matt. 18:19). 'Until now you have not asked for anything in my name. Ask and you will receive, and your joy will be complete' (John 16:24).

For one of our Christmas outreaches to Mexico, each of us needed $120. We told no one of the need, but only the fact that we were going to Mexico for an outreach. Ten days before the money was to be in hand, I had hardly received a penny. Then slowly some money began to trickle in. It seemed impossible that I would receive the full amount. I recall wrestling in prayer. Finally, a day before the deadline, I had just half the amount needed but I sensed that I had 'prayed through'. Though the tangible amount in hand was discouragingly little, somehow the Lord had given me a deep peace that the remaining $60 could come in the next twenty-four hours.

I woke up the next morning still feeling this peace. I started to offer the Lord a prayer of petition and then caught myself – I had the answer. I had nothing to ask him for; I could only offer praise and thanksgiving. God had already answered, though I did not know how. Later that morning I went to the student post office, where we collected our mail. I saw a friend there and, just before opening my mailbox, I told him there was a cheque in the box for $60 or more. And there was!

Training Worth More than Gold

How many times has something like that happened in my life? Once! So atypical of how God usually works, but God does at times give us very special indications to let us know that he really is there. Our faith is strengthened to trust him for something truly significant in life.

What about others who prayed for that $120 and did not receive it? Some Christians first receive their 'bachelor's degree' in God's graciousness in answering prayers in very clear (sometimes dramatic) ways and then go on for a 'master's degree' in God's mysteriousness. Others do the courses the other way around. For most of us it is a mixture all the way – quite a roller-coaster ride. How many prayers have I and other OMers prayed that are on the unanswered list!

Though theoretically our financial policy followed the guideline of 'information without solicitation', we realized that giving someone information often amounted to hinting for funds, which we saw as worse than solicitation. Many OMers, therefore, avoided all mention of financial need. In the 1980s some in OM questioned our policy. Does not Scripture teach us that biblical characters made financial needs known and quite clearly appealed to believers to help meet these needs?

We wondered if part of the reason we reacted negatively to fund-raising was that some individuals and groups have done it in a distasteful way. 'Tele-evangelist' has become a dirty word in some circles. Many sincere Christians conjure up an image of someone who is more interested in raising money than imparting spiritual ministry. Other fund-raisers may well be honourable ministers of God's Word but engage in a form of emotional manipulation to get the hearer or viewer to give above and beyond what she or he should.

These reflections came at a time of financial struggles in OM. As we looked back over two decades, we saw two clear testimonies in the area of finances:

First, God had met our needs. If you were to add up all of our expenses and all of our income, you would find they balanced out remarkably. Think of the thousands of people who have participated in OM outreaches and the hundreds of millions of pieces of literature that have been distributed. Our donors have been scattered all over world. Most of them have not had the foggiest idea how much anyone else was giving and yet, over the long haul, the credits equaled the debits.

Second, there were times when we fell behind in our payments. For most of the first twenty years of OM's annual conferences, we had the principle that we would not send out year teams from the conference until we had paid all bills up to date. Again we realized that if God were not in our efforts, it was better to let the mission dry up before embarking on a new year. A consultant who came to us in the 1980s to help us through a financial crisis remarked repeatedly that OM had one of the best financial controls he had ever seen: when the debts mounted, we cut back.

To put our debts in perspective, I do not recall that we ever owed an amount to anyone that caused our Christian testimony to be put in question. Almost all overdue debts that I know of were literature debts. The publishers whom we owed were very understanding. They saw that much of the difficulty revolved around the fact that people were not buying books at that particular time in the areas where the OM ships were operating. Under these circumstances, the publishers would rather have had their books on our ships than to have them sitting on their own shelves. They knew that they would eventually get their money – and they always did.

Still, this caused great soul searching. We had moved, without really analyzing it, from taking courses toward the 'bachelor's degree' in answered prayer to graduate courses in the mysteries of God. It was good for us in many ways. It was also painful. When finances are tight and you have to choose between paying bills or giving families the money needed to live as they believe they should, relationships are tested. We did not always come through the testing victoriously.

Trusting in Biblical Guidelines

These struggles were an added incentive to go back to the Instruction Manual and see if we were trying to be more spiritual than the Book. As we searched the Scriptures, we saw a biblical balance in raising finances for worthy causes. On the one hand there was God's intervention. But there was also man's responsibility. God works through His people in the area of finance, as He does in every other area of life.

Exodus 25:1, 2: 'The Lord said to Moses, "Tell the Israelites to bring me an offering. You are to receive the offering for me from each man whose heart prompts him to give."' The response was 'more than enough' and finally Moses gave an order that the people should not bring any more (Exo. 36:5–7).

Paul commended the Corinthians on their giving and exhorted them to complete the commitments they had made: 'We urged Titus…to bring also to completion this act of grace on your part. But just as you excel in everything…see that you also excel in this grace of giving. I am not commanding you, but I want to test the sincerity of your love by comparing it with the earnestness of others…And here is my advice about what is best for you in this matter: Last year you were the first not only to give but also to have the desire to do so. Now finish the work, so that your eager willingness to do it may be matched by your completion of it, according to your means' (2 Cor. 8:6–11).

The outcome of our Bible study on resourcing the work of God was the realization that there was biblical precedent for making specific needs known. There were also examples in the Old and New Testaments of asking in an appropriate way. Moses' petition in the Old and Paul's in the New treated the donors with dignity and honoured their freedom of choice. There was neither excessive playing on emotions nor manipulation. It was done in a sensitive way.

As we put ourselves in the shoes of the donors, it made sense. Certainly if we are to be responsible in our giving, we want to know the facts. It is good stewardship when incurring any financial expense to ask the hard questions. We should do research to see if the monetary outlay is a worthwhile investment. If we do this in the secular realm, how much more should we do it when investing for eternity?

Did it take less faith for Moses and Paul to raise funds by asking the people to give? Definitely not. The Bible makes no correlation between the amount of faith and the choice of method used. The correlation is between faith and obedience. What matters is obedience to God.

When we do any form of ministry, we combine faith and works. Evangelism does not occur if we stay on our knees all day. Yet evangelism will be ineffective if we never get on our knees. There is a need for kneework and footwork. The same can be said of preaching, teaching, discipling, counseling and raising needed funds.

Over these four decades, some well-meaning supporters of OM have referred to George as a great man of faith. Anyone who has met George, heard him speak, or read his writings, knows that George considers himself a struggler. He sees himself and all his co-workers as examples of the truth that it is better to possess a weak faith in the Lord Jesus Christ than to have a strong faith in anyone or anything else. We are thankful that God's work ultimately rests on something much more than our faith. It rests on his faithfulness.

OM's history is not a parade of servants who have been faithful, but a continual experience of his faithfulness in the past and the present. As for the future, we look forward to seeing him, the Faithful and the True. 'I saw heaven standing open and there before me was a white horse, whose rider is called Faithful and True' (Rev. 19:11).

Dale Rhoton has been with Operation Mobilisation from its inception in the late 1950s. He has led OM teams in the Middle East and Central Europe. Since 1978 he has been in the ship ministry, fifteen of those years as the director of OM Ships. He is presently promoting the ship ministry in North America. Dale and Elaine have three adult children.

Section 2

The Bottom Line in Mission Work is People Work

The bottom line in mission work is people work... loving them, serving them and helping them become strong disciples of Jesus.

George Verwer

Can Hurting People Be Fruitful Missionaries?

Allan Adams

Great biblical, mountain-moving faith does not happen without doubts, struggles and discouragement or even sin. It happens in the midst of those things. When we claim the cleansing of the precious blood of Christ, renew ourselves through the work of the Holy Spirit and come back to the cross, He will enable us to obey His commission to take the gospel to others.

George Verwer

During thirty years in mission I've listened to many missionaries and felt their pain. Our topic begs an initial question, 'What do we mean by hurt?' The spectrum of hurt includes anything from pain as a part of living in a fallen world to psychological disorder. Being hurt is an occupational hazard in missions and facing the suffering of a needy world further impacts the missionary.

Hurt is Real and has Real Consequences

Hurting people may seemingly function well, even in leadership, but the pain surfaces sooner or later. Relational and environmental hurts in their field of service are layered on the pain of the past. Some even choose more difficult distant places hoping to escape their pain and find solutions.

Poignantly, one man described his frustrations and disappointment,

> I didn't know I was hurting going into missions, to join OM was a challenge, a desire, and I was excited. I was hit blindside by the hurt that gushed uncontrollably out of me one night, triggered by a combination of things but mainly by an honest question 'How are you?' Not knowing the cause or end result of such outbursts, I pressed on. I pressed on until I could go no further, and that came about five years later. I threw in the towel. I blamed the daily frustration and confusion on culture shock. However, during the second term my familiarity with the culture didn't allow me to blame the culture and situation; in general I was more angry and destructive, especially toward my wife.[1]

Some fairly common sources for pain amongst missionary candidates include dysfunctional families, childhood abuse (including sexual abuse), adult children of alcoholics, issues of adoption and divorce, sexual identity problems, previous sexual behaviour including abortion, and previous demonic involvement. Occurrence in Christian families is similar to non-believing families. This continuum describes the spectrum of effects.

Healthy —— Bruised —— Dysfunctional[2]

While it is recognized that today's missionaries need more help because of the brokenness of their background, it is simplistic to imply previous generations were stronger and more immune to the effects of pain and hurt.

'Our parents might not have expressed a need for care but the pain was felt in their children's lives,' said one mission leader. He went on to talk about his own family; his father is a pioneer missionary leader who did his best for the family yet sacrificed for ministry. His children paid a price, the oldest son in particular.

There is pain in every generation, from the very beginning of humankind. The pain of Adam and Eve echoes down the generations; the pain of the curse of the Fall; pain from familial strife; the pain of tragic grief.

Everyone Experiences Pain

So the question is, 'Why are some hurting people fruitful and others harmful in ministry?' It comes down to what we do with the hurt we carry. Some live by denying the pain. Others live to dull it. Some cope by defining themselves primarily as victims. Many live with a determination to never get hurt again, often choosing to live in relational isolation as the only safe option. Some create a theological framework to support their denial, self-protection and/or pursuit of relief. These responses, when unchecked, can lead to harmful dysfunction.

Some hurts go deeper than others, penetrating deep into the soul. Some hurts require superhuman faith to expose because they threaten the person's very existence. They question the character of God, especially His goodness and faithfulness. Their exposure risks vulnerability to the opinions and judgment of others, especially those in authority.

We get excited about the stories of workers with all kinds of burdens and hurts bringing people to Christ. But we have to consider the lasting impact of the hurting missionaries on the believers. Are they replicas of the wounded missionary in outlook and theology? Is their understanding of God limited and anaemic? History is replete with examples of national churches taking on the characteristics, both positive and negative, of the founding workers.

It is sadly possible that hurting people cause more harm than good in missions. Such people would do better to work toward resolution of their unresolved pain before being sent into missions.

'Wounded People Wound People'

So says Kelly O'Donnell, clinical psychologist who works with YWAM and Mercy Ministries International and co-chairs the Member Care Task Force of World Evangelical Alliance's Mission Commission. He continues, 'There is a need to identify the kinds of problems that affect our workers and develop a protocol for dealing with people with significant problems – using the three S's.'

Screening – assessing overall maturity, both strengths and weaknesses; recognize significant psychological, physical and emotional conditions, and know what to do.

Support – developing a support system for those who are a part of the organization, a responsibility that includes adequate internal support and networking with external specialists.

Separation – identifying conditions that preclude service on the field, and help the individual move on to restoration and sensible placement.[3]

Kelly stresses, 'I believe each organization has a responsibility to develop structures and guidelines for each of these areas.'

Kelly presents clearly defined priorities of what is needed and how effective care can be given.[4]

Wounded leaders damage people. Unresolved hurt in the life of a leader is transmitted not only into his ministry but also onto his team. Hurt is a factor that can predispose to insecure leadership where vulnerability is threatening and trust is conditional, abuse of power is common, identity is confused with position, anger is projected onto others and 'others' become the cause of the problem resulting in the 'cause' being removed. The on-going cycle produces dissatisfaction in the team and keeps hurting people.

Wounded people create wounding organizations. Our core values are often aspirations of what we'd like to be and may not accurately describe the organizational ethos that influences the quality of life of our people. We must be able to look beyond the individual level of peoples' problems and assess the organizational dysfunction. An honest and corrective look at how we handle people is a prerequisite to organizational health.[5]

In our task-oriented, event - and experience-focused pragmatism (does it help get the job done?), peoples' needs easily take second place; in fact people can leave feeling bruised and used.

God is in the Business of Redemption

Much in Scripture says God uses hurting people in fruitful Kingdom ministry. Paul had a thorn in the flesh, David's sin had very painful consequences, Moses exhibited a serious lack of confidence, the woman at the well had only the testimony of her pain being touched by Jesus, Peter struggled with his inconsistency and legalism, Abraham was a man of faith, yet given to fear, Jonah was angry...and the list goes on.

Knowing and experiencing the God who redeems is the common theme in their stories. And examples abound today as well. One couple shared in their newsletter a story of vulnerability and hurt from the challenges of a less than easy lifestyle:

> Our return home was at a time when the accumulation of many years of stress had brought me to a standstill. Looking back over the preceding years I could identify many incidents, not only the police hassling that culminated in our arrest. Slowly my confidence that God was on our side was eroded.

> The stress of our personal situation, including the birth of our baby and his illness requiring urgent medical care, wore down our physical and emotional resources. My heart cry of pain and bitterness turned towards God. Everything was falling apart for us. Rising doubts about God brought me to the breaking point. I even wondered if He existed.

> Returning to our home situation was a significant new beginning for me. God slowly showed me what was in my heart. He also showed His father heart towards me. God gave very practical demonstrations of His care for me. I found a new understanding of His love and in the midst of this I could face the hardships of the last years. I found release and healing.

> I come to understand that ministry has to do with the inner man. Ministry is the outworking of what God is doing in my life!

The Gospel Addresses our Wounds with Hope

Those who dare to walk the path of vulnerability and transparency leading to personal healing are amongst the most fruitful missionaries I know. One whose ministry bears witness to his own healing wrote:

Coming from a damaged background I have been tempted to think I could never lead a fruitful, godly life. The need for acceptance and approval, aggravated by being orphaned and abused, clouded the simple truth of God's redemption. God and I have had our discussions wrestling with questions, Where were you? When? How could you let that happen? As I strained to look through that darkened glass, one truth became clearer: He died to make it right. The effects of pain, fear, grief, hatred and bitterness are not beyond the reach of the cross. I know this for a fact in my own life.

Serving in missions for the last twenty years, mostly in a country racked by civil war, I have shared my story and watched the simple message work its way into the hearts of hurting people. I have seen hope in the eyes of the hopeless, bitter hearts break in forgiveness and the guilty find pardon. And in that sharing I too have received, as transformed lives fill me with renewed joy and hope for the future.

Pain Makes us Move

Just imagine: you are hammering a nail and the hammer slips. Pacing up and down, you're volubly releasing the emotion that pain evokes.

Pain drives us in a direction. Many choose anger, bitterness and revenge. We try to stimulate or sedate ourselves with some form of addiction to make us feel better, to find a way of coping. Many addictions are disguised or dressed up acceptably, even drawing praise. Over-work, hyper-activity, travel or even coffee appear innocuous whereas others are more sinister (alcohol and pornography) – yes, even missionaries are susceptible.

A Place to Go

Jesus stood in our place of guilt. He took the judgment that was due to our sin. The Cross is a place of substitution—that we understand. We know how to take sinners to that Place.

Jesus identifies with our pain as he suffered in exactly the same ways as we do. So we can tell people that he understands. This brings comfort that he knows and understands. But pain needs more than empathy and identification. It's not enough to tell a hurting man that I understand his pain because I'm in the same place. He wants to know what to do with it!

Isaiah in chapter 53 prophesies in poetic but profound words that Jesus carries our sorrows; he takes our pain on Himself. This is where we go, to the Place where pain is healed. The Cross is a Place of Transfer for our pain and woundedness.

This is surely not new or unknown. It is not theological word play; not spiritualized platitudes or a laser-beam instant cure. Jesus became flesh and dwelt amongst us, touched us and entered into our lives. And we bring healing to others with the same incarnational touch, anointed and directed by the Holy Spirit. Walking the path of his woundedness with him, we sensitively yet decisively lead the hurting one to that Place.

A dedicated lady whom I respect for her pioneering spirit shares her story,

I knew I'd had quite a deprived childhood, with a distant father and a busy mother, and I knew this might have something to do with my difficult relationship with God, but I was not able to do anything with this knowledge.

I went to seminars, poured out my heart, in the hope that I would find the right answer. Normally I came away with the assurance that I was okay; it was 'normal'. Over the years I became more and more desperate and convinced that something should change, and at the same time it looked less likely that anything would ever change. This affected my work; I became exhausted and it was just my will power and routine that kept me going.

God took me by total surprise in my home country when I was invited for a talk with a Christian doctor. I was convinced my problem was spiritual and not emotional, but I accepted the offer. God used this talk to get me in touch with the pain inside of me. I suddenly saw in my mind a child that had hidden herself from the world, crouching in a pitch-dark, huge cellar. I knew it was me and I faced this pitiful, frightened child. I saw Jesus come in and take this scruffy child in his arms. She was no longer scruffy, but a beautiful chubby, pink toddler. And I could hear Jesus' roaring laughter, full of joy and love.

Not everyone will have exactly the same experience. Meeting Jesus is distinctively individual but the underlying principles are the same.

Jesus Set the Priority

In his hometown synagogue, Jesus is handed the Scroll of Isaiah. Intentionally reading chapter sixty-one,

> The Spirit of the Sovereign Lord is on me
> because he has anointed me
> to preach good news to the poor
> He has sent me to proclaim freedom for the prisoners
> and recovery of sight for the blind
> to release the oppressed
> to proclaim the year of the Lord's favour...

He did not finish the sentence and rolled up the scroll. All eyes were fixed on him. Very simply he made his personal ministry statement: 'Today this scripture is fulfilled in your hearing.'

That's what he did for the next three years, nine o'clock Monday morning as he 'walked into his office', on his time off and indeed wherever he went, he touched, healed and set people free.

Helping Hurting Missionaries is Crucial

Many missions today are acknowledging the need for ministry to hurting missionaries, but experience shows these moves are not readily understood or accepted. Wary about becoming too introspective, some fear we'll lose sight of the Goal. Setting people free to think for themselves and draw their own boundaries threatens some leaders. Could it be a similar reaction to that of the religious leaders in Jesus' day? Healing people upsets the status quo.

Missionary exegesis with the emphasis on 'going' and 'reaching the world' is over-developed in comparison with dealing with people's needs. We come up short in a practical theology that gives real answers for woundedness, with implications also for the people we serve.

Why all this emphasis on healing? Does it not lead to self-absorption? Over the years I questioned myself, Why the reticence towards such ministry? Surely the purpose of healing is not to focus on the experience. Being healed we are set free to focus on our purpose and calling; we are more able to do what we are set apart to do. Never is it our intention to change the nature of our organization into some kind of AA support group. Our goal is healthy people who can face the dangers and struggles of the front lines.

Developing a Capacity to Endure

'Resilience is an added component to health, one that is essential in those who live and thrive in cross-cultural ministry,' says Laura Mae Gardner, International Coordinator for Member Care, WBT International and SIL International.[6] She goes on to describe resilience as the capacity to bounce back, to withstand hardship and repair oneself. It is the creative ability to live on more than one level at a time. In a world where disconnection, dislocation and disorganization seem to be prevalent, you need to be resilient.

She outlined indispensable building blocks to ensure the 'making rather than breaking' of the missionary in his cross-cultural context where change, disruption and loss are often inevitable.

- Building a foundation of beliefs about God that can weather the assault of a crisis and that can allow for injustice, disease, genocide and the like whilst not minimizing his Sovereignty and Goodness.
- Deliberate and intentional development of relational skills especially for cross-cultural relationships without neglecting relationships from home. Such broad-ranging relationships give perspective to life and belonging. Loneliness is a slow killer.

- Accurate risk assessment: assessing the likelihood of encountering change and crisis and making adequate plans to deal with these in a healthy way.
- Assessing the estimated personal impact and making anticipatory preparations for the unexpected, unpleasant and unplanned change.

Missionaries Carry the Pain of Others

Integral to being agents of change through the power of the Good News, missionaries are subject to stress, loss and trauma, and confronted with poverty, death and injustice.

A doctor in West Africa commented: 'I walk through the grief cycle every time I tell a patient that he has AIDS. And I have to do this daily. Grief is a part of my everyday experience.'

A burden of grief, even despair, can descend as they identify with overwhelming, endless need. This process is called secondary traumatization, also known as vicarious traumatization, compassion fatigue, and has symptoms similar to burnout. This condition is ubiquitous.

There are three risk factors:

1. exposure to the stories (or images) of victims,
2. the worker's own empathic sensitivity to their suffering,
3. unresolved personal emotional issues that relate to the suffering seen.[7]

Learning a lifestyle of 'transfer', regular debriefing along with practical stress management and proper relaxation are measures that need to be addressed both by the worker himself and by the leadership.

Fruitfulness in Missions Entails Suffering

Even a superficial understanding of mission history, beginning with Paul's experience, will lead us to acknowledge that suffering is a part of missionary life.[8]

Engaging in the travail of incarnation and redemption essential to fruitfulness does demand a dimension of wholeness. Unresolved pain and unhealed brokenness will usually tend towards self-absorption and self-protection that hinders spiritual productivity.

In the shadow of his hour of greatest suffering, Jesus established the benchmark in a simply practical yet profoundly symbolic act.

Wholly man, he is secure in his identity, destiny and relationships, and convinced of his purpose. He, who knows pain like any other, knows the source of healing.

He steps forward, takes off his outer garments, wraps a towel around his waist, stoops down and washes their feet.

'I have set you an example that you should do as I have done for you.'[9]

From 1974 until 1988, Australians Dr. Allan and Rhonda Adams served on OM's ships Logos and Doulos including five years as director on each vessel. Concurrently they pioneered the ministry of OM in East Asia. Allan was OM's regional Area Coordinator for East Asia Pacific until 1995. Based since 1989 at the OM Ships headquarters in Germany, Allan works on a consulting basis with leaders and conducts courses in leadership development, member care and personal development. Allan championed member care in OM, and helped establish the Oasis Counselling Services in OM Conferences. They have three adult children.

---

[1] The examples in this article are mostly OMers or former OMers who gave permission for their stories to be used. Personal details have been altered to ensure anonymity. The first man mentioned is not in the same situation today. He returned home and sought help, his family is stable and healthy, and he considers further service.

[2] Esther Schubert, 'Current Issues in Screening and Selection', p. 74 in *Missionary Care*, Kelly O'Donnell, ed., Pasadena: William Carey Library 1992

[3] Kelly O'Donnell, 'Wounded People Wound People', in *Doing Missions Well: Member Care Within and From Africa* compiled by Kelly

O'Donnell for the Association of Evangelicals in Africa, Mission Africa Conference, Ivory Coast, May 12-16, 2000

[4] Kelly O'Donnell 'Going Global: A Member Care Model for Best Practice', pp. 13-22 in Kelly O'Donnell, ed., *Doing Member Care Well*, Pasadena: William Carey Library, 2002

[5] Kelly O'Donnell and Michelle Lewis O'Donnell, 'Understanding and Managing Stress' p. 110 in *Missionary Care*

[6] Laura Mae Gardner, 'The Making or Breaking of Missionaries: Promoting Resilience on the Field', Pastors to Missionaries Conference, Dec.1999

[7] See David V. Baldwin website {www.trauma-pages.com}

[8] Colossians 1:24 – 2:5

[9] John 13:1-17

Suffering and Missions

Jonathan McRostie

We seem to have a strange idea of Christian service. We will buy books, travel miles to hear a speaker on blessings, pay large sums to hear a group singing the latest Christian songs — but we forget that we are soldiers.
George Verwer

Suffering is part of the Christian mission movement. The Bible teaches that serving God faithfully here on earth includes adversity. The early Christians suffered greatly as they carried out their Master's mandate. History shows us that mission work has always been accompanied by suffering.

Operation Mobilisation is no exception. Perhaps because of OM's characteristic mobility, travel brought suffering on several occasions. From my own personal involvement I mention a few. After my first four years in OM Europe I left for a visit to the USA. Arriving in New York, I was greeted with the news of an accident. Just days before in Zaventem (near Brussels), I had sent off in prayer Keith Beckwith, OM's leader for the UK, and John Watts, leader of the literature ministry STL. Both died in a car crash in Poland. In one blow we lost our British leadership.

Yugoslavia in the 1960s claimed more than its share of pain. Ron and Nan George were early leaders in Europe and the Middle East. Returning from Iran to England in a VW van, Nan suffered a spinal injury that left her hemiplegic. Her story is recounted in *Treasure In Jars Of Clay*. Despite years of mobility limitation, God has used Ron and Nan to pioneer work in Muslim lands. For the last ten years they have led a vital development and training ministry, World In Need. Another van accident in the same era involved six young people, all potential long-term leaders, returning to Europe from India. God took four to himself: Chris and Hillevi Begg, Sharon Brown and Jay Sunanday. The two survivors, Fritz Schuler and Frank Fortunato, are senior leaders in OM today. I spoke at the memorial service for Sharon Brown in Montana, USA. Another brother and friend, Tony Packer, suffered a few months imprisonment. Neither Yugoslav hospitals nor prisons were very humane in those days.

In the early 1970s I coordinated Europe from Italy instead of the headquarters in Zaventem. Tragedy struck the Zaventem team. Margaret O'Malley, a university graduate, served well on the team in the accounts department. A gas leakage contributed to her drowning in the bath. I remember speaking at her funeral back in Liverpool and seeking to comfort her parents and church.

1982

I was in Spain with my family, visiting teams during Easter. I attended a missions conference near Barcelona, focusing on outreach to the Muslim World. I recall speaking to former OMers and recounting events of that year. In January, a Dutch brother Joop died in Adana, Turkey, of heart failure (his sister told me that the family suspected possible poisoning). News from Bombay in February told of a fire that wiped out records, literature and damaged the premises of OM India's headquarters. In March, word came of Swiss brother Willy's truck accident in southern Sudan. Because of the isolated territory, he died beside the road before any medical help could arrive. I wondered out loud to my friends, 'What might happen in April?'

Three days later I got my answer. I had driven with Pedro and Trevor to visit Portugal and appoint an OM representative. En route back to Barcelona, we had an accident near Guadalajara, Spain. I suffered a broken neck which has left me paralyzed, functioning in a wheel chair ever since. I did not ask what might happen in May!

Certain memories stand out about that event, which God used to keep me going. While in intensive care, Daniel Gonzalez, OM leader in Spain, came to visit. He had lost his wife Lily to leukemia a few months previously. His question to my wife Margit was: 'Do you have peace?' We could say 'yes' because God had given his peace in our hearts. Another OM leader, Mike Evans from France, came and proposed a communion service. Margit and I and Mike remembered the Lord at my bed in intensive care. They had to put the bread in my mouth as well as the cup to my lips. That probably was my most memorable communion! Other people helped in a tremendous way, and the family stayed incredibly loyal. How we appreciated George Verwer's concern and moving 'heaven and earth' to mobilize prayer as well as action to get the best care and rehabilitation for me.

Why?

Only God in his infinite wisdom knows completely why all kinds of sufferings exist. My experience is more with physical suffering. However, a large part of mission suffering is disappointment with those who make a commitment to Christ and then fall away. I remember spending hours with Michel, a French fellow on the Zaventem team. In spite of all the input, Michel, who had a previous prison record, later ended up in prison for attempted murder. So much for seeing a faithful man develop! Broken relationships can cause even more hurt which, in my view, is more agonizing than a broken neck.

The root of all the evil and suffering in the world is the fall of mankind. Why did God create us with the possibility of such a fall, influenced by the powerful temptation of Satan? Joni Eareckson Tada gives some good thoughts on this subject in her book, *Diamonds in the Dust*.

Does God cause blindness or does He allow it? Does He plan for a person to be born deaf or does He permit it? In short, does God want the disease? The key here is how we use the word 'want'. God doesn't want disease to exist in any sense that He enjoys it. He hates disease just as he hates all the other results of sin: death, guilt, sorrow, and so on. But God must want disease to exist in the sense that He wills or chooses for it to exist, for if He didn't He would wipe it out immediately.

But most important, God is delaying closing the curtain on suffering till more of the world can have the chance to hear the Gospel. For if God erased all disease today He would also have to erase sin, the general cause of disease, and that would mean the destruction of all people. It is God's mercy that delays His judgment! 'Though he bring grief, He will show compassion, so great is His unfailing love. For He does not willingly bring affliction or grief to the children of men' (Lam. 3:32–33).

Does God ordain? Permit? Allow? The verb is not so much the important thing as the noun: God. And God is love.[1]

The mission Christ gave us to take his good news to every creature is the greatest answer to the problem of suffering. Most suffering is not just 'by chance'. It may seem so, but the vast majority is caused by human factors. Buildings that are built by cutting corners to satisfy greed end up collapsing in an earthquake, thus producing more death and destruction. Most evil is caused by human beings. For someone suffering a spinal injury, the pain of rejection by friends and/or family hurts more than the actual disability. I met such people when in rehabilitation. The gospel brings inner healing, enabling us to trust God to further his purposes in the midst of difficulties and setbacks. It brings us his comfort, knowing that he has identified with us in our suffering. To follow the example of Christ, we too must suffer, personally and on behalf of others. As suffering and comforted servants we can then offer comfort to others.

How to Respond

Negative reactions produce more evil and pain. Bitterness and blaming others, even God, poisons our lives. Some despair to the point of hopelessness and even suicide. How we respond is more important than what happens to us in life. Mission history furnishes countless examples of positive attitudes in the face of trials, which have resulted in the advance of the cause of Christ. Unfortunately, we probably are all acquainted with the opposite as well!

It is far better to be realistic and *accept* the adversity with confidence in God, knowing he is in control. But acceptance is not sufficient; we also need to *act*. For me, this meant obtaining good care and therapy. I also needed to co-operate and do exercises that would ultimately benefit me. Forgiving and not blaming the driver who fell asleep in our Spain accident has contributed to a healthy friendship between us over these years. Positive action includes thinking of and serving others, rather than wallowing in self-pity. Having a God-given purpose in life is great therapy for a paraplegic! To *learn* from our suffering requires asking what God wants to say or teach us. He may show us some of his purposes, but he alone knows how much explanation we truly need. One lesson that I have learned through suffering is to be more understanding of others who suffer. As a young energetic man, I used to think the flu was just a cold, and could not understand why people would stop working. Then I got the flu! My accident has rendered me even more sensitive towards people in pain.

Helps to Continue

Confidence in God who is sovereign, all wise, good and just

Joni expresses it well.

> God is exalted as head over all-including peace and war, light and darkness, health and sickness, prosperity and calamity. Someone once said that Satan may power the ship of calamity, but God steers it to serve His own purposes. And when it comes to God's purposes, we have His promise that nothing will be allowed in our lives that is not for our good or that is too hard for us to bear (Rom. 8:28; 1 Cor. 10:13). But when we say that God allows Satan to do the things he does, it isn't as if Satan twists God's arm and God hesitantly grants permission. Nor are we to imagine that once God grants permission, he nervously runs behind Satan with a repair kit, patching up what the devil has ruined. The Lord is never forced into a corner. The Lord is

never backed against a wall. Not only is God never frustrated or hindered by Satan's schemes, but God actually uses the devil's deeds to advance his kingdom and bring glory to Himself.[2]

Contemplation of God's compassion

Meditating on Christ's incarnation, suffering as a human being, weeping at the grave of Lazarus and in Gethsemane before the crucifixion – this brings great comfort. God has identified with us in our weakness, that is why he can give comfort – encouraging strength to endure even as he did.

Commitment to our calling

As disciples we are called to follow both the Master's instructions and example. The priority is not seeking a comfortable life but obedience.

Considering models and mentors

I am stimulated as I read realistic mission biographies and stories of mission groups. What an encouragement to see God use very weak people! God also has overruled mistakes, divisions and sin on the part of mission workers – including us in OM! I led the work in Britain in 1963 in the midst of many doubts and struggles. Yet God raised up 700 recruits, clearly reflecting his grace in furthering his purposes through weak people.

We also need to consider mentors who are usually people we know. Miss Jones, a teacher I had at a school for missionary children in West Africa, is unforgettable. Some forty years after I had seen her, I telephoned her at a Florida retirement home. It happened to be my birthday. I said, 'Miss Jones? This is Jonathan McRostie.' She instantly replied, 'Oh, Jonathan! Today is your birthday and I have been praying for you!'

Stephen Hart, for many years the chief accountant of OM based in Zaventem, exemplified faithful prayer for teams around the world. How much he rejoiced whenever they saw fruit. He also taught me to see the positive and not the negative in people. When someone would begin to criticize a mission or worker, Steve would quickly begin to list the strong points of that work or person.

I also think of Dr. Homer Payne who served God in the French speaking world in Switzerland, France, Belgium and Quebec. What a help he and his wife were to my wife and me in the early days of our marriage. Now at the age of ninety-one he continues faithfully serving the Lord in evangelism and discipleship. Such models and mentors are an immeasurable help in our pilgrimage.

A community of colleagues

What a privilege to be part of a community of not only co-workers, but also genuine friends. I pay tribute to George Verwer for his loyalty, humility and care for his fellow workers as much as for this hurting world. George is a truly great communicator – by telephone, prayer, conversation, letter – and his friendship has helped me enormously. In 1963, during my time of many doubts concerning the veracity of the Gospel, I thought George would send me home. Instead, he stood with me in my struggles.

A few years after my accident, I was very discouraged because of my frustrations and negative thoughts and words. I was to visit OM's ship *Doulos* in Spain, but felt utterly unworthy to go and speak for God. At that moment, George telephoned me from England and asked how I was doing. 'Not very well,' I replied. After my explanation, he asked, 'Who is telling you these things?' Of course, I realized that it was not God. Maybe it was myself, but my mind did not usually give me such discouraging ideas. It must have been from our adversary, the devil. George's reply was very brief: 'What the devil says is a lie!' As a result, I did go and minister on the ship in Bilbao.

Conclusion

Suffering may seem to interrupt or hinder our progress in accomplishing the mission task. But by God's grace, suffering can serve to mold our character and deepen our compassion. Therefore it is for our good. Certainly suffering will serve to further the glory of God. He is the one who has commissioned us, and will accomplish his work in and through us. Is all of this easy? No! Is it possible? Absolutely!

Jonathan McRostie has been with OM since the early 1960s. For over twenty years he served as European Co-ordinator. The past twenty years he has ministered from a wheelchair due to a spinal injury in 1982. Married to Margit from Germany, he has three grown children who are married. Presently he directs internationally OM World Partners — a fellowship of former OMers. He is also involved with the European Disability Network of Christian disability ministries, serving on the Steering Group

---

[1] Joni Eareckson Tada, *Diamonds in the Dust* (London: Marshall Pickering, 1993), p. 51

[2] Eareckson Tada, p. 52

Mothers in Mission

Lenna Lidstone

The Holy Spirit does not wait for all our cultural baggage to disappear before he can use us in a powerful way.

George Verwer

My husband Julyan and I spent fifteen years in Turkey with Operation Mobilisation. The work amongst Muslims who made up 99.9% of the population had begun in earnest when OM sent two workers in 1961. Other mission agencies followed but, when we arrived in 1980, there were only about fifty believers from a Muslim background and a similar number of Christian workers.

Despite Turkey's secular constitution, mission activity or 'Christian propaganda' as it was called was a heinous crime and the authorities were quick to dismiss from secular jobs and deport anyone they suspected of ulterior motives. Security was tight and no one really knew how long they would be allowed to stay.

Julyan and I had met at Bible college in Glasgow and married, knowing we would be heading for Turkey the following year. Our vision was to be involved in church planting and we set out for Ankara with great zeal, anxious to be used by God and determined to stay as long as he would keep us there.

Yet when I returned to Scotland a year later for the birth of our daughter Emma, I remember the sense of relief as I boarded the plane. A tangible weight of language and cultural adaptation rolled off my shoulders. It had been a hard year. I felt ill-prepared to fit into this male-dominated society and regretted my seeming lack of bent towards domesticity! Maybe instead of complementing my teaching experience with two years of Bible college, I should have studied home economics or at least learned to knit. My attempts at Turkish cooking had been as embarrassing as the knitting.

Language classes had been a nightmare. I'd thought that being pregnant wouldn't affect my learning but I felt so sick most of the time and especially when travelling to our course, packed like sardines in a smoky bus. My fat Scottish vowels always brought scowls of disapproval from the teacher. Turkish sentence structure is completely back to front. No wonder it gave me a headache! Being in the same class as Julyan wasn't always helpful. He was such a natural and took it all in his stride, so much so that I was shocked when I had the unsanctified temptation to scribble all over his vocabulary notebook.

Hard though it had been, I knew that God had called me. Even before Julyan and I had got together I knew that. I reminded myself that this venture into mission had been God's idea and I determined to allow him to put his arm of encouragement around my shoulders in place of any self-imposed burden.

Mentoring through Motherhood

Motherhood, however, brought new challenges. Long, unexpected water cuts and electricity failures were more troublesome when there was loads of washing to be done. There were constant visitors. My role continued to be focused on the home with lots of practical serving and an ongoing sense of inadequacy.

Life seemed full of tasks that I didn't do very well. Any gifts God had given me were lying dormant. My weakness with language meant that I felt just a fraction of myself in my new culture and that people didn't really know me at all. An English-speaking Turkish friend with whom I could share everything kept me from despair.

It was in this context of what seemed like personal death that I watched God bring a church into being. People were coming to faith and there were no church buildings or suitable local venues where the believers could gather. It was in homes including mine where the church grew. Looking back, it was such a privilege to use these early years of motherhood to care for my children and also facilitate God's work.

I didn't always see it in this light. I wrestled with issues of privacy, the personal time and space that my independent spirit demanded. Often I felt we were living our life in a goldfish bowl where our relationships were so exposed. It was hard to hide sinful attitudes. My attempts at compartmentalizing 'family' and 'work' as though they were separate callings left me emotionally exhausted.

During a particularly tough patch when I was feeling resentful that I had to share my home and family with so many others, I was reminded of the birth of our daughter. She had been rushed back into hospital with a high temperature when only a few days old. For three days she underwent painful tests. Of course I stayed with her, praying without ceasing. God linked in my mind a mother's longings for her child and God's longings for a young church. It changed my outlook on life in his service.

That day as I felt God's heart like a mother's, and mine a pale reflection of his, I realized that God would use who I was and what I had to offer for his kingdom purposes. Being a woman, a wife and a mother in what seemed like a man's world would not be a restriction at all but rather the gateway into wider ministry.

For our Turkish friends who had come to faith in Christ, it was vital that they were welcomed into the Christian community and that they felt part of the family of God. They needed warm loving relationships – not just attendance at meetings. We had no choice but to have an open home. I realized that true discipleship doesn't come from a book but through shared lives. It was important for younger men and women to see Christian marriage and family life modeled by us, imperfect though we were.

As the years passed the work grew and our international, interdenominational team in Ankara became intercontinental. The East Asians, Latins and South Africans had arrived. Within the wider foreign mission family we had every flavour of theological persuasion. God had lots of scope to rub off our rough edges. Sometimes it felt as if I'd been turned inside out and cleaned with a scouring pad!

God used this close community to change us and teach us how to really love one another. I learned that intimacy in relationships comes through the fellowship of suffering. When the Turks and foreigners were rounded up and held by the police in 1988, a tremendous bond was forged both inside and outside the cells. A Turkish mother and I were in contact every day sharing our fears, encouraging each other with scriptures and praying. Relationships were so rich. I don't believe we've experienced fellowship like it since.

Sometimes it was hard to be a mother and not have an older woman around to look to for advice. We were in a pioneer situation and most of us were in our twenties and thirties. I still marvel at the way in which God sent people to me when I really needed help.

God's Guests

On one occasion we were particularly concerned because Emma had developed a stammer which lasted several months. At just the right time, a co-worker's mother arrived from America. She was a speech therapist and was able to give us wise and reassuring advice.

Schooling for the children was always an issue and the question of what next was never far away. When we lost our residence permits because of police harassment, we knew registering in the school system would not be allowed and that deportation was possible. Just at that time we were visited by an older couple whose children had grown up in a variety of mission situations. Again the wise motherly counsel of a more mature Christian mother brought peace to my heart and I was able to give the burden back to God and trust him for the next step.

The answer to our schooling difficulty was me. I reminded God that I had left school teaching and gone to Bible college because I wanted to teach the gospel and not mathematics. I learned that, for mothers in mission, the need very often is the call especially if our own children are involved. At the time it seemed like a deeper death for me but it facilitated the beginning of a school that would grow and develop after I had moved on.

I always appreciated visits from our mission leaders. They saw me as an important part of the team. Even if I was busy with the children I was encouraged to join in discussions as I was able and my ideas and opinions were always taken seriously. In a country where women are considered less than equal this attention was most welcome. These men had time for our children and even their pets! They were great models of servant leadership and when their wives visited with them it was even better.

We had so many interesting people stay in our home. I remember the late Lionel Gurney, founder of the Red Sea Mission Team, who even in his eighties continued to travel in the Middle East. When he stayed with us he would recount his exploits as a missionary doctor in Yemen at the breakfast table. Our children, Emma and Samim, particularly enjoyed the story of the boy whose bottom had to be stitched because he'd been bitten by a crocodile.

Soul Satisfaction

Now aged twenty and seventeen, they love to reminisce about their childhood and regularly pore over photo albums. They enjoyed our lifestyle in a country that knew little of bedtimes and babysitters. They always felt included whether it was amongst the mission workers or the local Turkish church. Turkish came easily for them once they made friends for themselves.

As the children grew we moved to Izmir. Julyan's leadership role involved a lot of travelling. Often I was left at home 'holding the fort'. Then there were the times I travelled back to Scotland on my own with the children. It was never easy occupying them for hours in airport lounges. They did learn patience, however, and became very good at amusing themselves.

In Izmir I home-schooled Emma and Samim and we were able to do some trips as a family to other cities and countries where Julyan and I began to minister together. Our final years were spent in Istanbul. Here I was asked to speak at a Turkish retreat and teach a short course in child development at the small Bible college. At last, I was able to transfer my communication gift into the Turkish context, but now we were in our fifteenth year and preparing to return to Scotland!

Over the years there were many things on my heart to do for God that I couldn't do. God raised up other people to do them and I learned to rejoice in the accomplishments of others and God's work being forwarded. I learned to think 'we' and not 'I', and to be engaged in God's purposes from my heart. I found that by supporting others in prayer I really did become a stakeholder in God's work.

This was brought home to me forcibly once when my children were sick with whooping cough. I was unable to attend a field retreat that I had helped to organize and had been looking forward to for weeks. God ministered to me from Psalm 63 and I found myself again in love with him and he with me. I discovered at a deeper level that God wants my heart more than anything I can ever do for him. My experience at home had paralleled the message of the retreat. God's Spirit is not restricted and he didn't miss me out. Actually, it's impossible to miss out with God if he owns your heart.

The Deborah Dynamic

You don't have to be a mother physically to feel God's motherlike heart towards his people. There are many single and married women without children who have birthed ministries, gathered the saints and nurtured young leaders.

We read in Judges 5:7 that Deborah arose a 'mother in Israel'. She was moved with righteous anger because of the oppression of the enemy and had faith that God could change the situation. She's a good example of mothers and mission going well together. People working with street children and orphans often burn with a similar passion.

Perhaps she's also a good model for any missionary agency wanting to be a prophetic presence in a land and seeking to call out national leadership to mobilize a church. Deborah like any mother with her own children loves to see them find their niche and do God's business. We can see how her faith inspires and challenges, rebukes and encourages. She overflows with pride in God's people when they do well and she sings her praises to God for his victory, giving him all the glory.

To be a spiritual 'mother in Israel' we must learn to 'sit' under the palm tree, like Deborah did. In the Bible palms are associated with victory. We need to rest in the victorious work of Christ, so that our hearts can tune into his. Where is this place?

In Judges 4:5 Deborah's palm tree is situated between Ramah and Bethel. These names have rich connotations in the Old Testament. Rachel, another mother in mission, was buried near Ramah. Jeremiah 31:15 says that the sound of Rachel weeping for her children is heard in Ramah, weeping as the exiles pass by on their way to Babylon. This is quoted in Matthew 2:18 where Rachel is again heard weeping, this time as Herod massacres the baby boys around Bethlehem.

We have to live within earshot of Ramah. Unless we are conscious of people living in exile, dying without Christ, and at the same time experience the weeping mother heart of God, our praise will be hollow and triumphalistic. However, we need to find our shade near Bethel too. This is the place of dreams and visions. In Genesis 28 we find it to be an open Heaven where God meets with Jacob. At Bethel he promises far-reaching blessing and fruitfulness beyond what we could ask or think. Without Bethel, we'll give up.

Mothers in mission is not something we do; it's something we become. It's a calling for life wherever we are. We intercede, not withdrawing when things get tough but pushing through the pain to a healthy birth. We nurture through encouragement, always believing in our children. With teenagers the issues are when and how to let go. I'm learning the importance of the strong relationship and good open communication developed through the childhood years. These lessons are probably vital for mission agencies too who are working with national church plants. Teenagers need the freedom to make mistakes.

Mothers mustn't smother. Jesus rebuked his own mother at the wedding in Cana and he rebukes us too when we become dominant. Mary had the wisdom to humble herself and urge the servers, 'Do whatever he tells you.'

I guess that's what all mothers in mission really covet for themselves and their children – hearts that put God first and obey Christ.

Lenna Lidstone met Julyan at Bible college in Glasgow. They married and in 1980 went to Turkey where they brought up their two children, Emma and Samim, and were involved in church planting with Operation Mobilisation until 1995. After some years in pastoral ministry back in Scotland they have returned to Operation Mobilisation as area co-ordinators for the Turkic and Persian world.

Leading Under Risk of Failure

Humberto Aragão

Failures for the believer are always temporary. God loves you and me so much that he will allow almost any failure if the end result is that we become more like Jesus.

George Verwer

Those who want to reach the top of the mountain must assume the inherent risks. Latins, however, prefer to avoid uncertainties, risk and especially failure. They express their unease with uncertainty through emotional expression as a means of acceptance, hard work in order to save for the future, and a need for laws and rules.

At the same time, Latins admire and follow those who display integrity by risking themselves for the benefit of a cause. Successful people in society – regardless of their field of endeavour – are different than average people. Their lives are marked by discipline and commitment to their visions and dreams above all else. Their convictions are related to objectives and goals often established early in their lives. They acquire knowledge and training related to their objectives. And they are well aware of the risks resulting from their choices as they reach for their goals.

George Verwer has been a great example of a risk taker. He has shown the world what the power of a vision given by God can perform in lives of people. It was – and still is – a risk to establish a ministry depending only on the conviction that God is willing to use young people from around the world in a new wave of mission enterprise. All the time and effort in prayer, thought, strategy and implementation have caused him pain, sorrow and loss, but his inner convictions both of the needs of this world and the values imprinted by God in his soul and heart have kept him steadfast.

In missionary ministry the risk of failure will always be present. Once God confirms a spiritual vision to a leader, he must initiate the risk of practical implementation of those truths that govern his soul and mind. Invariably this will produce pressure, stress and pain beyond the imagination. Only then will the leader's knowledge and training, together with the inner conviction of God's vision, determine the quality of results.

In times of tremendous stress and crises, our convictions, integrity, loyalty, determination, assurance and capability for suffering will be tested. Those tests will reveal who we really are, and if we are ready to assume the risk of implementing a new vision, ministry, or task. The external elements of a leader's vision − the strategy, goals and programmes − will suffer all kinds of criticism, jealousy and envy. We will need to explain every step of the way to reach our goals. The maturity with which we receive criticism will build solid ground for growing relationships.

For many leaders, the implementation of a vision has been costly. Some of my own family members firmly rejected my standard of living and involvement with God when I began my ministry with Operation Mobilisation. Some that were very special departed from our circle of friendship because of our commitment to the reality and high price required. However, if we faint not, more people will be infected with our example.

The Risk of Failure

My first ministry as pastor in a small church was marked by failures. I failed in the way I communicated with the leadership. I thought that I could be the answer for the problems in the church. I couldn't understand why deacons and elders were asking questions about my character. Weren't the goals I had for the church bringing results? I caused bitterness, broke relationships and lost people so precious to our ministry. I was legalistic in my way of seeing others and their ministry. My vision of others was measured by what I would do. My concept of commitment was measured by my own abilities to stick to an expected result. I failed in my understanding of God by not admitting his mercy and grace upon others making mistakes. I thought that maturity would come together with conversion, and that people learn transformation by the power of God – without much self-discipline.

It took a good time of learning through painful experiences until God started to work deeply in my life to restore what I'd lost. A new understanding of my humanity and God's love, mercy and grace came upon my heart and soul. To discover a God bigger than my failures was the great finding in life. To see others not as source of problems, but for their potential in the hands of God, became a must in my life. All of us live with various fears, but none is as crippling as the fear of various kinds of failure.

Risk of Failing with God

When I decided to join OM's ship *Doulos* in 1979, I left a good profession as a chemist in a large steel company. For two years I would be absent from the cultural symbols that identified me as a person. I had to speak another language without prior knowledge of it. I had to change my job as a chemist working with an x-ray spectrometer to peeling onions for the crew in the galley. The chances for failure in my new position were greater than in my former job. Many of my most important lessons were never learned formally in a school or a church's discipleship manual.

There was a day when the lesson became so hard that my old bad nature, supposedly dead and crucified with Christ, was ready to step down from the cross and punch my leader in the nose. I had to clean up under the stove in a tight, sticky, greasy place. In this leader's language there was no 'please' mentioned in conversation, which made it very difficult for me as a Latin man. I became furious, fighting against my inner convictions and desires. My inner convictions regarding becoming a man of God to a world without God had been shaken and tested. Through those crises, I evaluated my motives and convictions in relation to the goals I settled upon before joining that blessed ship.

When we face such situations, our hearts cannot understand what is really happening. It is easy to lose direction and not perceive the precious practical lessons awaiting our learning. At this point the risk of failure will be at the door.

Risk of Failure with Family and Relatives

Many businessmen today are exchanging their homes for their jobs. Forced to choose on a practical, day-to-day basis between their spouses and families and their jobs, often careers win. Even in ministry we can lose precious relationships because of weak inner convictions regarding God's plan for family priorities. I recall that many times in my youth I made my parents suffer because of my foolish and misplaced zeal. I could make people feel out of the will of God if they opposed my thinking. It was hard to consider a mistake especially in public. My ministry made me blind to the motives of others, their love for me in different ways, and their concerns for God's kingdom. In reality they were right in many ways, and I was wrong in my perceptions.

The good news is that many people whom God has used made mistakes and failed their families. Abraham lied twice, affirming Sarah as his sister, out of fear of the king. He slept with his wife's servant, in order to help God provide an heir. Noah drank so much that he shamed his sons by his nakedness. David failed with God as he murdered a man. Mark failed with his uncle Barnabas as he returned home and left the ministry. All these men failed God but were not abandoned by God. As they responded in repentance, God restored them. Failure is not the main problem, but what I do with my failures. What lessons does failure teach me?

Risk of Failure with Friends

Friendship for a Latin is very special. We love to make long-term friendships, and wherever we go, hospitality will follow. Friends will never set an agenda or schedule to visit; friend are always there for each other. Latins like to live around people, to touch people, and embrace people. They learn to live and work for themselves but also for those dear ones. There are friends closer than a brother or sister. To fail with a friend will damage the whole atmosphere at the place of ministry, work, or school.

This cultural value makes it easier for Latins to adjust to cultures with a similar worldview. As far as friendship is concerned, they get along very well with Central Europeans, Asians, Middle Easterners and Africans. But no matter how good our friendship might be, the risk to fail with friends is there. Most leaders whom God has used in history failed their friends when their vision of God was at stake. When choosing his team, Paul had a horrendous argument with Barnabas over John Mark, and their relationship was at best strained.

Yet how many friends we can drive away from ourselves and the Lord through zeal without wisdom, or speaking plainly without love and grace. I remember times when I was defending myself instead of simply recognizing my mistakes, letting others help me to rest in the Lord. God had to work in my life through adversities to show my dependence upon him and others.

Being humans and sinners will lead us to moments of failure with friends. The good news is that God can forgive and restore our relationships. When Abraham recognized his sin and failure before the Lord God, he was restored. When David recognized his sin against God and man, God restored him. When Mark recognized his sin against God and man, God brought him back into the ministry. When Paul developed his spiritual life through painful experiences, God restored him into a long-lasting ministry with Barnabas and John Mark. The risk of failure with friends is part of the development of a good leader.

I have met leaders that have difficulty acknowledging people around them because they have yet to learn to deal with their own weaknesses and God's grace. Other leaders are on the verge of losing families due to their zeal for their ministry. Their wives cannot understand a God like this, and are ready to quit their relationships. Some leaders move from place to place because their wives are unwilling to listen to the criticism heaped upon their husbands. Remember that God is at risk in giving us our ministry; He is the most interested to restore our failures with brothers and sisters.

The Risk of Loneliness in Ministry

Latins live close to parents, relatives, and friends and thus fear loneliness. Our culture exists for the collective group. We feel emotionally drained to work with people who deem friendship as unimportant. When I joined OM India I was young and full of dynamism and energy for preaching the gospel; as a person, I was full of opportunities to grow under pressure. I had the chance to learn about the Indian culture, social life, costumes, arts and music. I wish I had then the mind I have today, for I would better approach those precious moments in India which, upon reflection, were the best months of my ministry life. During that year I would cry alone in my room, missing dear ones, the jokes from my friends, the places I frequented at home. Initially, everything in India was new to me and exciting. Then the reality of staying for almost a year hit, and all the values imprinted in my soul bombarded me. Lack of letters from those whose said they loved me. Lack of finances from those who said 'Go and we will lift you up here.' Lack of solid disciplines that could hold me up in times of distress. All my training and formal seminars could do nothing for my loneliness.

In my first ministry as pastor in a small church, I had one of the most painful experiences in my Christian life. A moral problem involving people in leadership whom I loved caused great spiritual stress. I could not sleep for nights, crying alone and with the Lord. It seemed that my strength was gone. All my knowledge of problem solving learned at seminary did nothing to help free me of loneliness. It seemed as though God decided to be silent with me. I felt like a victim, called to suffer for the ministry of that church. Yet step by step God formed his team that, together with me, solved that situation without the destruction of any family or division in the church. Those with maturity and sensibility to work with people came together in prayer and fasting, asking for the mind of God upon those problems. I experienced the beauty of the body of Christ in times of crisis.

It is Worth the Risk!

There are moments when due to difficulties, lack of finances, lack of infra-structure or lack of human resources we lose our good soldiers. Moments when it seems that only you are still fighting a war that cannot be won alone. Moments that we have only the cross and the heart to search for answers to continue. Moments like these can lead to despair. In the movement I serve, I take great joy in sitting with leaders from politically resistant fields. They share their sorrows, experiences, turmoil and pains with me – but also their joy and happiness to see people coming to know the Lord Jesus Christ. Their stickability and willingness to pay the price, to take the risk and come back even after failure, is worth it for the eternal joy it brings.

Humberto Aragão began his missionary career with OM's ship Doulos *in 1979. After studies in the Baptist Theological Seminary of the South in São Paulo, he served for one year with OM India. Since 1993 he has been the national director for OM Brazil, serving as well as pastor of the First Baptist Church of Jardim Morumbí in São José dos Campos. An author of two books on leadership, he also teaches in the Haggai Leadership Institute.*

Growing Leaders for 2020

Viv Thomas

Could you imagine the apostle Paul with a cell phone?

George Verwer

George Verwer, for as long as I have known him, has always been committed to leadership development. Over the last forty years he has used every resource available to spur and occasionally cajole his fellow OM leaders towards leadership development. The project has been successful in many of its dimensions as there are leaders throughout the world who are in his debt due to George's contribution to their lives. Yet, his thoughts about leadership have always been in the context of disciple making. For George, a leader's primary qualification is to be a disciple of Jesus. The measure of good leaders to him is one of their walk with God and not primarily their gifts, charisma, ambition or influence.

There is little doubt that George's desires around this subject have been right, but the questions of what sort of leaders are needed for the future and how to develop them is an open one because the variables are many. Different times demand different types of leaders; what looks like great leadership in one set of conditions can be inappropriate in another. We have to carefully watch how we grow leaders because ultimately leadership is about power. Styles of leadership promoted and developed in the West in the 1940s will not work well in this new century in a trans-cultural organization. You cannot drop Canadian leaders into North India and tell them to lead or vice-versa. What works at one stage of an organization will not work at another. Leadership development must keep moving, particularly with all the challenges offered through technology, globalization and post-modernity. Our task is not easy and needs to be worked through with boldness, imagination, cultural sensitivity and wisdom.

Models Which Become Blind Alleys

Before we can answer what sort of leaders we need to develop it is worth looking at a few blind alleys which evangelicals are walking down in their search for good leaders. The first one is what I call *Conservative-Evangelical*. All that leaders need to know is the Bible; the more they know of the Bible the better leaders they will be. This is a good idea but inadequate, because knowledge of the Bible does not mean knowledge of God – even if you can do a really good exposition of Biblical text and call yourself an evangelical.

The second blind alley is what I call *Charismatic-Prophetic*. Leading is to do with the feelings associated with the moving of the Spirit. 'Spirit-led' leaders will know the mind of God and, through their feelings or an impression regarding what God is saying, they will be able to lead. It is also good but the dangers are self-indulgence, tendencies towards totalitarianism and lack of discipline.

The third blind alley is what I call *Contemporary-Cultural* model. The emphasis is on cultural relevance and communication. The great shame is to be behind the cultural pace and therefore irrelevant. Leaders are to be seen primarily as communicators. From this another set of problems arise. If you merely focus on the culture and relevance you become thin in your approach. You have no substance because the point becomes the *communication* of the message rather than the message itself. Image triumphs over substance and all that is left is an empty and hollow shell of leadership.

To learn how to understand as well as teach the scriptures, to hear the voice of the Spirit and be contemporary in our communication are all-important for leaders. But to pursue one of these alone unnecessarily narrows the vision and will lead to poor leadership. Over the long haul a deformed church and organization will result.

Instead, we need leaders who have a relationship with God, do their tasks with skill and commitment and have healthy relationships with themselves and others: spirituality, task and community.

Spirituality: Relating to God

Leadership is about relating to God. Without this understanding a Christian leader is the SS *Titanic* steaming towards an iceberg in the dead of night. You can relate to God in joy, anger, frustration, humour, praise and silence but you need to relate to him. Yet to do well in this, you first find that there is no fast track or 'efficient' way to a life of relating to God. Many have learned all the right Bible verses and principles but have developed little in their understanding of God or personal maturity.

Secondly, you learn that God is in control. Leader types like to control, build and envision. It is difficult to accept that Christian leadership is about inadequacy not adequacy. This marks us out from our contemporary secular brothers and sisters who begin with human potential, while we begin with human inadequacy and see what God will do with it.

Thirdly, you can put yourself in the way of God through the basic disciplines of the Christian life. You cannot control God but you can be ready for his initiatives.

Fourthly, developing a knowledge of self. John Calvin said that the two crucial issues were a knowledge of God and a knowledge of ourselves.[1] We have often lived with the fantasy that we can know God without knowing ourselves. This is particularly dangerous for the followers of leaders who have no knowledge of themselves. Leadership is not just about knowing God but about knowing who we are. They are two sides of the same coin.

Task: Doing What You Do Well

Organizational leadership is about change: the transformation of something into something else. Leaders are intended to make a difference through influence or impact as they engage in tasks which will produce change. This may be short- or long-term but change is the focus, regardless of how long it takes.

It is startling what people can learn if they really want to. So many of the skills needed can be learned: how to do what we are intended to do; how to contribute to helpful change; how to treat the Bible properly to teach and not abuse it; how to develop a strategic plan; how to motivate people and empower them; how to integrate new technologies into leadership structures to handle work well and maintain a contemporary sharpening edge. It is pivotal that we develop organizational cultures of lifelong learning to grow and flex with each new situation.

We can also learn to develop that most central characteristic of leadership: vision. All leaders are not necessarily visionaries but all leaders need some sort of vision. This can be learned through correct exposure to God, the world in which we live and the bringing of the two together.

Herein lies the Christian leader's danger. Aiming to complete tasks can lead into a world of control. Such can be the focus on the task, such can be its all-consuming power that it has to be completed at all costs. If leaders only engage with God and their own skills, they can tumble into power fantasies and ideas which are totalitarian at the root. This often happens without them being aware of the process or the result. How can we avoid this particular danger often demonstrated? How can we avoid addiction to the task dominating everyone in the name of God and causing considerable damage? The answer is not in merely doing the task but in engaging the community.

Community: Living With Your Friends

This is where the great shift has to occur to have the right sort of leaders developed over the next decade and connect with the generations of leaders to come. This is especially so for leaders brought up within a Western worldview.

I was eating lunch with a few Christian leaders and one asked, 'What would you pick as the one main characteristic of people who are leaders?' I answered, 'The ability to make friends and sustain loving relationships.' The answer did not impress my lunch partners and, while I was speaking the answer, it did not impress me. For leaders are to stride the globe, create dynamic organizations and cultures, are they not? Making friends and sustained loving relationships sounds weak in the presence of contemporary leadership ideas. Yet, I am convinced that it goes right to the heart of leadership because of the nature of God.

God is community, three in one and one in three. His power and authority in producing creation and redemption all come from a God who is not the isolated 'one' distant from relationships. He is the Father, Son and Spirit who are in eternal and mutual love towards each other. His power comes out of this eternal community of love with himself. If leaders are to reflect the image of God in all they are and do, they must reflect this in their relationships. A leader who cannot develop and sustain friendships of loving communion with others will ultimately be destructive.

Character as Building Blocks

How then can we develop leaders who are spiritually mature, do what they do well and can sustain loving relationships with others? We can note four key areas as a basis for growing leaders.

Firstly, *we have to see leadership formation through the lens of spiritual formation*. It is not enough to take secular models of leadership, baptize them with Christian enthusiasm and vocabulary then let them loose on an unsuspecting church. The result will be disaster. Eugene Peterson has noted the problem when Christian leaders simply take the values and goals of secular leadership and lead. The values of consumerism turn the church and her accompanying organizations into 'a company of shopkeepers'[2] and abandon their call and 'while asleep they dream of the kind of success which will get the attention of journalists'.

To be spiritually formed means that leaders are in the process of becoming fully human, growing in all that God has intended them to be in the various dimensions of life. Money, sex, prayer, emotion, culture, discipline, politics, vision and many more areas fit under this idea of spiritual formation. Our mistake in the past has been to merely focus on a spirituality of lofty feelings of goodness and pious sensibilities, which has led to a rejection of the material reality of our organizational lives and has caused endless confusion and continual problems. Leadership has to be approached from the spiritual formation of all that we are before ourselves and the world in relationship to the love of God expressed through his word. We can then go on and take leadership models from others, but frame them in the context of what they do to our own spiritual formation and the shaping of those we lead.

Secondly, *we need to see the development of leaders who can listen*. Leadership is often seen from the perspective of the power of the leader who can communicate well so that people know how to dialogue with the leaders they choose to follow. Yet the key to being a good communicator is being an even better listener to the many messages which surround. Developing leaders will mean teaching a series of questions which will be continual and lifelong. What is God saying to me through my friends or those I perceive as enemies? What is going on beneath the surface of this person or organization? Why am I really doing what I am doing? Listening to God through revealed scripture, listening to your own heart, listening to friends and the culture you are in, and listening to the Spirit's voice through all of this is at the core of developing leaders. Great leaders are great listeners.

Thirdly, *we need to engage an open life of vulnerability and avoid a preoccupation with image*. Leadership is surrounded by the myth of the super-hero defying all odds through extreme circumstances, not only surviving but flourishing and receiving every accolade from an adoring public. Yet it is not real. Super-heroes do not model leadership reality and the mythmakers in Hollywood and Bollywood know it better than we do.

Leadership comes from humans who interact appropriately with their world. They look at the world in which they are called to live and seek to live for God in its midst. Leaders who lead well engage with reality, entering into a dirty world and becoming dirty in the process. Developing leaders who know how to be vulnerable in the realities of their own lives is crucial for the Church.

Linked with this is *image*. In our increasing obsession with image, reality is often ignored or understood as how we appear rather than how we are. Repentance is not needed in a world where image dominates; a new surface replaces the fading old one and suddenly we are free. Yet, image is important and one key to developing leaders is the creation of the right image – not a series of masks or faces for particular audiences, but rather a response to the image of God offered to us through creation and redemption brought about through the Cross. This demands vulnerability and an openness to let the image be made by God and not ourselves. There is no problem with image if it reflects the reality of what is inside.

Fourthly, *we need to develop leaders who are generous*. Leadership is about generosity, the ability to give and keep on giving. This will work its way through into an extravagant belief in people. If a leader does not believe in the people they are called to lead then much is lost. We become mere functionaries of organizational life. This characteristic of generosity is underplayed and yet is foundational to a Christian understanding of leadership. Developing leaders will necessitate teaching potential leaders how to give themselves along with their time and resources to others. Leaders who see the church as a series of competing tribes and work from a narrow sectarian frame will tend towards meanness. This is opposite to the love and generosity offered to us in Christ through the Holy Spirit.

In conclusion, we are called to develop leaders who know God, can do their tasks well and be in continual interaction with the community. The leader must be well-formed spiritually becoming fully human as God intended, be adept at listening to God, themselves and the world, able to live with their own weaknesses and process them well without running for the cover of some illusory image. Leaders must be generous in order to lead well. This is not an impossible vision but within our grasp if we encounter God through his word and listen to the Spirit. Only after this can we then go on to our training courses, mentoring programmes, leadership retreats, reading schedules, hard targets and all the other décor of leadership development.

Dr. Viv Thomas is a leadership consultant and author of Future Leader *and* Second Choice. *He speaks throughout the world on leadership and spirituality and is a visiting lecturer at* All Nations Christian College *in England and Briercrest Seminary in Canada. He has been a member of OM's International Coordinating Team for eighteen years. Viv, who resides in London with his wife Sheila, received a PhD from King's College, London. You can contact Viv through his website {www.vivianthomas.com}.*

---

[1] John Calvin, *Institutes of Christian Religion*, Henry Beveridge, trans., (Grand Rapids: Eerdmans, 1989), p. 37

[2] Eugene Peterson, *Working the Angles* (Grand Rapids: Eerdmans, 1987), p. 2

Section 3

The Greatest Missions Movement in History

The greatest missions movement in history is taking place right now. You'd have to be dumb to think this stuff isn't exciting.

George Verwer

Global Missions and the Role of the Two-Thirds World[1] Church

Joseph D'Souza

I am sure that God is already using many of you more than you realize. Be aware of the subtleties of putting yourself down in an unbiblical way, just as I am sure you would beware of allowing yourself to be puffed up. Be aware that God is doing great things in the world today. He is working through older churches, newer churches, older agencies and newer agencies in an exciting way.

George Verwer

The Global Church is in the Midst of a New Era

Today for the first time in history the church has a global face. Whether it is the eighty million Christians in China, the masses of crypto-Christians in India, the dominant presence of the Church in the African continent or the explosive growth in Latin America, the church is alive, strong and growing in the two-thirds world. This is at a time when, depressingly, the church in most Western nations is in an advanced state of decline. Numerically today more than sixty per cent of the global church is found in the two-thirds world. Given both its population and the rate of church growth it will not be long before the vast majority of the Christian church will be non-Western.

A similar majority of workers involved in evangelism and mission work among those who do not know the gospel are from the two-thirds world. Post-colonial realities of national independence and ownership of national institutions forced indigenous churches to own responsibility for their churches and the evangelization of their world.

It is impossible to get an accurate picture of the number of two-thirds world workers in missions. The most recent edition of *Operation World* says that there are about 44,000 Indian missionaries in India.[2] However, growth has been so rapid that there are close to 100,000 workers involved in presenting the gospel in India today.

Another example is the immigrant worker 'evangelist-missionary' from the two-thirds world found in the Middle East, Europe, USA and Central Asia. A huge number of Filipinos, Indians, Chinese, Koreans and Latin Americans are spread among the unevangelized – migrant workers carrying enormous zeal and commitment to evangelize. This is not different from the growth pattern of the first three centuries when dispersed believers took the gospel from the street (public preaching), to the home (house churches) and to the palace (crypto-Christians in high places).[3] Persecution and work opportunities were two reasons why Christians were dispersed among all sections of the population. Michael Green tells us that even in Paul's time the gospel had reached the rulers.[4]

A difficulty in missions literature has been that Western-type mission organizations have been the main platform from where much of evangelical missions thinking and initiatives have come in the modern missionary era. Although the church itself is to be the direct vehicle of missions, it has concentrated on theology, not missiology. This has an inherent weakness because the church does not in actuality become the primary agent of missions.

However, today two-thirds world church mission movements are the platform from which most current missions initiatives and reflection will come. These movements within China or Korea[5] (a good example of the role played by the church, not missions organizations), the Pentecostal and non-Pentecostal Church movements of Latin America, the African Independent Churches or the underrated and underestimated Pentecostal and independent evangelical Church movements in India are examples of this reality. This paradigm shift is a huge and welcome change, because it is always the Church which must be the primary vehicle of carrying out God's mission on earth.

The Two-Thirds World Church and its Mission Context

The AD 2000 and Beyond Movement's most important contribution has possibly been the highlighting and popularizing of the massive challenge in the 10/40 Window. The prism of the 'unreached people group' has been used extensively as a strategic tool. But this can turn out to be an 'exotic' description of people because it tends to sanitize the hard contexts and changing realities in which people live and evangelization takes place.

The crucial fact is that the two-thirds world church is not only located among the larger percentage of the world's unevangelized, but also faces the most complex and difficult challenges in world mission. Not enough attention has been given to these hard realities. Factors such as the massive population explosion and socio-political realities in the two-thirds world make the task as challenging as ever. A few major contexts need serious consideration.

Hostility

One of many forms of hostility facing missions is that *Christianity is connected with colonialism.*[6] For the people of Asia, Africa and even Latin America, Christianity is still synonymous today with colonialism, even though there have been many evangelical missionaries in a number of nations who were the prime promoters of national independence.[7] The impression that the West was Christian when it colonized the world and is still Christian has not changed.

The rise of religious fundamentalism, the current global political atmosphere and the huge media discussion about the clash of civilizations only reinforces the common prejudice. This is further confounded by the negative aspects of globalization, especially in the growing economic disparity between the rich West and the poor of the two-thirds world – seen as a form of economic colonization by the Christian West.

Even with the numerical growth of the church in the two-thirds world, the church is not significantly active in society to counter the common perception that *the West is Christian, so Christians must be like Westerners.*

This challenge can only be met by evangelical churches in the West and the two-thirds world church in their respective societies countering the perception that the ills of Western culture are due to its Christianity. Surely if Islam can launch a worldwide defense that Islamic extremists do not represent true Islam, the call to change the common perception of Christianity is not just a fantasy!

Another aspect of hostility is that 280 million Christians live under persecution where religious liberties are constantly trampled upon and people are martyred for their faith. Nigeria, Sudan, China, Burma, India, Tibet and Indonesia are places where the church is contending with religious persecution and the taking away of religious liberties. Similar repressive moves are afoot in the CIS nations.

Religion as an integral way of life

The great religions of the world – Hinduism, Islam, Buddhism, Taoism, Sikhism – are thriving in the two-thirds world where religion is lived out as a fundamental way of life. Religion gives societies their roots, cohesion and community. It has helped people survive colonial oppression and rule. Religion provides identity, belonging and rich cultures that preserve family structures from the decline in sexual morals seen in the West.

It is also true, however, that religion has contributed to the ills of the caste system, idolatry, oppression of women, infanticide, superstition, temple prostitution, female circumcision, agnosticism and other destructive forces.

Western criticism of Asian religions has seen religion as a set of beliefs rather than a set of cultures. Asian people may be open to a critique of beliefs in the light of modernity and other changing contexts, but the offer of present-day Western culture in exchange for theirs has never been attractive.

It is mainly because of this that the Christian church has seen the least response. We do not have on hand the offer of a demonstrable, visible alternate religion as a way of life but merely Western cultural interpretations of the Christian faith and church models based on Western rationalism, highly dualistic and privatized. Only in the last few decades has serious thought been given and action been taken in order to create communities of believers within an

George and Drena

Moody Bible School students prepare for outreach in Mexico

One of the two groups that left for Mexico

George Verwer Snr., George and John Stott in 1992.

Area Co-ordinators of OM in 1994. Front, left to right, Dennis Wright, Dale Rhoton, Peter Maiden and George Verwer. Back, left to right, Rodney Hui, Bertil Engqvist, Mike Wakely, Allan Adams, Joseph D'Souza and Dave Hicks.

George preaching in Incheon, South Korea, in 1997.

George with former directors of the ships in front of *Doulos* and *Logos II* in 1994. Left to right, Peter and Bernice Nicoll, Dale and Elaine Rhoton, George and Drena Verwer, Dave Hicks, Mike Hey, Chacko and Rhada Thomas, Bernd and Margarethe Guelker, Gerda and Manfred Schaller, Mark and Esther Dimond and Allan and Rhonda Adams.

George at the opening of Urbana 2000.
Photo: InterVarsity/Twentyonehundred Productions

George with Barney Ford, Director of Urbana 2000.
Photo: InterVarsity/Twentyonehundred Productions

George and Drena welcoming one of the OM ships with
co-founder Dale Rhoton and wife Elaine.

Photo: Greg Kernaghan

existing set of cultures, since creating a new set of cultures is not an option.

Grinding poverty and its consequences

Whether in Africa, Latin America or Asia, most people live in unbelievable and grinding poverty and its consequences. The poor are both sinners as well as the victims of the sins of others. Illiteracy, unemployment, drugs, prostitution, AIDS, starvation, hopelessness, crime, and violent political movements run rampant among the world's poor.

This poverty is fertile ground for religious fundamentalism and terrorism that is the scourge of the world today. If the colossal amount of money spent on the war against terrorism in the last couple of decades had instead been spent on uplifting the poor in the areas where terrorism has flourished, perhaps the world would not have been pushed to the brink today by terrorists. Belatedly the world has realized that the conditions that give rise to the easy manipulation and brainwashing by figures like Osama bin Laden have to be also addressed if we are to combat religious terrorism.

Two-thirds world missions have understood that a holistic approach to missions among the poor is the only approach that maintains the integrity and credibility of the gospel and evangelization, but the work among the poor is daunting. The call to disciple the poor will take into consideration all areas of their life that need to be redeemed by the gospel – including giving them the tools and resources to live with dignity as human beings that are made in the image of God. Degrading and dehumanizing poverty among Christians does not glorify God and is a slur on the global Body of Christ.

Massive social and civil unrest

Two-thirds world missions in many places are confronted with massive social unrest triggered by religion, ethnicity, economic collapse, oppression of women, social injustice and political oppression. National churches and missions in these lands cannot be mute spectators. Christian citizens have the challenge of being light and salt in society to have relevance within their nations.

Take for example the massive caste unrest in India where hundreds of millions of people from the Dalit and backward castes want to break free from a social structure that has dehumanized them. The Dalit has no access to the temple or to God, and has been told that his present condition in life is due to God's punishment for sins committed in a previous life. In short, God does not love him.

Clear prophetic gospel statements of both word and deed by the church and missions in the public sphere (as opposed to closed-door Christian gatherings) articulating how the gospel of Jesus Christ sees these people is the need of the hour and will have immense impact on the decisions of hundreds of millions of people in matters of faith.

Or, take the example of ethnic conflicts among Christian ethnic groups. Does the Church have anything to say or do to halt such genocide? Wherever such events occur it impacts evangelization and the long-term relevance and credibility of Christians.

The Two-Thirds World Church and Global Missions Cooperation: Critical Issues

Globalization, for good and bad, is impacting the world[8] in education, technology, travel, economics, information and the media. Cultures are clashing and assimilating simultaneously. The movement of personnel, information and technology around the world is putting incredible pressure on all cultures to change and adapt.

Two contrasting events capture some of the critical points in the new world. The first event was *the breaking down of the Iron Curtain and the collapse of the Communist Soviet empire*. Nations had to come to terms with a unipolar world where the USA became the predominant global power. The triumph of Western capitalism brought deep change in the economic realm and in the open access the West now had to the rest of the world for economics, labour and technology.

The second event that was both barbaric and deplorable is *the September 11 attack on America*. The message here was equally clear: the extremist sections of the Islamic world are not equally open for all things from the West – especially any social or political action connected with their religion.

In a unipolar and open world, there are sections of life where the powerful West must not interfere or take leadership. In other words, there are sections of life that are out of bounds for the outsider.

The critical issues the two-thirds world and global missions must consider will be impacted by the conflicting forces that are at work in our world: it is redundant to discuss the end of the missionary era and Western workers in mission. With the presence of mature two-thirds world churches and missions, new paradigms are necessary for global participation and cooperation. It is the two-thirds world church that is now best equipped, in cooperation with the global Church, to fulfil the task of world evangelization. It is crucial that the leadership of the Christian faith and initiatives for evangelization among the unevangelized is firmly in the hands of two-thirds world leadership.

The open world of today will allow Western workers willing to adapt and function in the new context – not as missionaries but as students, professionals, businessmen, etc. Just as there is the dispersion of two-thirds world labour among unevangelized peoples, there is a dispersion of workers from the West. Church leaders in the West need to be aware of the potential of this avenue for evangelism and missions. Where missionary visas are still given, the key concept will be to work with and through national churches and workers. Where there is no local church the same dynamic principle is still relevant. Even the first group of new believers that come to Christ in an unevangelized group can become the base for working through nationals. Mission work needs to lead to the establishing of local churches placed in society to carry on their mission. Evangelization must take place from within society.

The rapid growth and availability of national workers in many parts of the two-thirds world tells us that we must invest resources, time and money to recruit, train and send out national workers through their local churches and mission groups. The support of nationals locally or internationally is not an either/or issue. You need both if you are serious about world evangelization in the present generation. Churches and leaders in the two-thirds world must determine how much of their local/national support is required at any given time so that their work will continue even if and when outside finances are no longer possible. This is for the leaders of the two-thirds world church and missions to decide, not outsiders. The deliberate campaign by a few in the West to stop supporting nationals is as destructive to the cause of world missions (if not more) as saying that Westerners should not be involved in mission work overseas. A global cooperation in financing, recruiting and sending out two-thirds world workers across nations into unevangelized areas is long overdue. It is embarrassing that Latin missionaries by the many thousands are unable to move to Europe, Central Asia and even the Middle East because their local economies cannot afford the cost of cross-cultural missions.

How does the global church hold the Christian West accountable for their acts of omission and commission in relation to the work of world mission? The information age has shrunk the world into a computer. Scandalous public actions, bad attitudes to people of other cultures, inappropriate terminologies and 'military' language in the public sphere in the expansion of religion can no longer be confined. Instant global communication accessed by anyone is part of the new world order. This could result in major attacks on Christians in places where they are a minority or cause huge stumbling blocks in evangelization or set back a mission project by decades.

The two-thirds world church missions movement needs to mobilize more financial resources within their nations for world evangelization. Self-support is a negative goal for our times. In many places groups and churches are satisfied that they are self-supporting, ending their missions program. The creation and mobilizing of resources for the evangelization of the masses around them are not in their thinking. Some church bodies have successfully seen the starting and running of businesses as a means of supporting evangelism.

The increasing rediscovery and application of the full dimensions of the gospel in the two-thirds world church need continuous study and analysis, and must then be shared intentionally with the global church. Two-thirds world missions is all about the Gospel as offering 'communion' with God through the forgiveness of sins in Christ; offering 'community' in society through the local expression of the church; offering the 'power of God' for bodily healing, deliverance from evil spirits and dealing with crisis; offering liberation from ignorance and dehumanization that occurs through poverty; offering 'prophetic challenge' to all that is evil in the midst of social upheavals.

Conclusion

The two-thirds world church needs to go back to the church of the first three centuries for answers to some of the critical problems and issues it faces. There are many parallels such as a minority church, a church under oppressive structures, a church that is self-theologizing, a church that is expanding, a church that faces an uncertain future, a church that has syncretism and a church that has to deal with the scandals of church history in which they have had no part.

There is no doubt that the two-thirds world church and missions are messy. It is the messiness of growth, movement and life. A certain amount of syncretism, problems with leadership style and succession, compromise in the midst of outstanding courage, and failure in the midst of development are all present in this section of the body of Christ. But how can self-theologizing leadership structures and styles that are right for the host cultures and gospel redemption in community and society occur without making mistakes and taking time?

Major national prayer movements back up the two-thirds world missions movement. With prayer as the major foundation of the growth of the Church in these lands, God will take care of the Church as it meets the challenges ahead.

Dr. Joseph D'Souza joined OM's ships in 1973 and upon returning to India in 1976 joined with OM India's field teams as the state director of Uttar Pradesh. In 1981, Joseph became OM India's training director, and in 1989 became OM's Area Coordinator for India. For the last thirteen years in his role as Area Coordinator, Joseph's main roles include providing overall leadership for the movement in India, casting vision for the work and giving pastoral care to his top-level Indian leaders. He and his wife, Mariam, have one son and one daughter.

[1] The term 'third-world' is out of fashion today. In the first instance it became pejorative in meaning. Second, with the collapse of the so-called second world (communist world) it lost rationale. The term 'South' is used by some to describe the people of the southern hemisphere but the geographical definition does not cover all the emerging churches and missions nations of the world. The 'two-thirds world' term is largely inclusive of all such nations and as yet does not have a pejorative connotation.

[2] Patrick Johnstone and Jason Mandryk, *Operation World: 21st Century Edition* (Carlisle, UK: Paternoster Lifestyle, 2001), pp. 2-6

[3] J. Herbert Kane, *A Concise History of the Christian World Mission* (Grand Rapids: Baker, 1978), pp. 3-35. Also refer to Stephen Neill, *A History of Christian Mission*, Penguin Books, 1964, p. 35.

[4] Michael Green, *Evangelism in the Early Church* (Grand Rapids: Eerdmans, 1971), pp.142-143.

[5] On May 25, 1995, the South Korean church dedicated 105,000 young people for at least two years of mission service. This is an example of church taking over the responsibility of mission

[6] Arun Shourie talks at length about this aspect in his book, *Missionaries in India: Continuties, Changes and Dilemmas*. He claims that the work of the British rulers, missionaries and the Oriental scholars as a joint effort '…to civilize India, to secure it for the British Empire, to gather it up as the rich harvest for the church proceeded as a joint endeavour: the civil servants helped by many devices, including among these their "religious neutrality"; "the soldiers of the Cross: reinforced each other's efforts; and the scholars helped working to "undermine" and "encircle" and thereby prepare the way for "the soldiers of the Cross" to "finally storm" "the strong fortress of Brahminism"'.

[7] M.M.Thomas, *The Acknowledged Christ of Indian Renaissance* (Madras: CLS, 1970), p. 243. Thomas mentions the role of C.F. Andrews with Mahatma Gandhi in Indian nationalism.

[8] There are number of articles written on this topic., e.g. M.P. Joseph, "Denying Life: Theological Meaning of Globalization", *National Council of Churches Review* CXVI, No.6, July 1996, pp. 453-68. According to Joseph globalization promotes the radical negation of God, a form of institutionalized atheism by erecting false images as God, rationalizing the death of many for the comfort and luxury of few. To the question of why globalization, Maria Mies, the famous

German environmentalist, recently said that if globalization is meant to raise the living standards of all the inhabitants of this earth to the level of the Americans and the Germans, then the resources of the earth are sufficient for only nineteen days of life. If the consumption rate of all are lifted to the level of the rich north and equalized, then we need seven more planets to live. K.C. Abraham writes that globalization in the third world leads to cultural invasion, ecological crisis and in the process the most affected are the poor, the powerless, women, children and the tribal people. Please refer to 'A Search for the Role of YMCA Amidst Globalization: Towards Building a Just, Participatory and Sustainable Society', *National Council of Churches Review*, Vol.CXIX, No.9, Oct. 1999 pp. 787-800.

Mission from Poverty and Under Pressure

Bagus Surjantoro

What we need are tasks in which we can see a combination of the 'possible' and the 'impossible'. We want to be filled with faith and be realistic. If you are discouraged by your 'humanness' in the face of the Great Commission, overwhelmed and paralyzed by the size of the challenge then consider for a moment Paul's approach to his weakness expressed in 2 Corinthians 12:8–10. We tend to forget that however filled with the Spirit we may be, there is still the human factor. We are ordinary people who struggle, make mistakes and have weaknesses. I have become more and more convinced that God fills and uses different types of people, many of whom may not look very promising by normal standards.

George Verwer

God does not bless the nations by using only one particular, rigid method but rather four different mission mechanisms: 1) going voluntarily, 2) going without missionary intent (involuntarily), 3) coming voluntarily, and 4) coming involuntarily (as with Gentiles settled forcibly in Israel; II Kings 17).[1] This shows us how serious God is with his mission: it does not depend upon circumstances or our economic, political or social well-being.

In my experience as a Christian from a developing country and – while writing this article – ministering with OM's ship *Logos II* in the Caribbean, I have encountered Christians who hold a different view. This ethos holds that mission must start from rich, established, civilized nations or that mission must be the job of affluent Christians and churches that are strong and wealthy. In real terms, mission is therefore the task of Westerners. This belief is mistaken.

Blessed to Be a Blessing

Every believer is blessed. The greatest blessing is salvation through Jesus Christ. Only when believers recognize that they are blessed will they fully understand God's mission as He said to Abram: 'I will bless you...and you will be a blessing...All peoples on earth will be blessed through you' (Gen.12:2,3 NIV).

Our God is not a cruel God who only commands service to Him. Instead, God blesses us to become a blessing. His blessing becomes a resource for our service to him. Only those who realize that they are blessed can be a blessing to the nations. Recognition of God's blessing changes our attitude from 'What can we get?' to the attitude of 'What can we give?' prompting us to be a blessing for our Jerusalem, Judea, and Samaria and to the ends of the earth. This commission to every believer − to be a blessing to the nations − is not based upon economic, political or social conditions, but upon the fact of God's outpouring of blessing on his children.

Sent Out or Kicked Out

Jesus spoke carefully about mission. Luke 10:1 says the Lord *sent* the seventy, two-by-two, using the word *apostello* and, in Luke 10:2, Jesus highlights the need to *send out* workers into His harvest field, using the word *ekballo*. These two different Greek words, *apostello* and *ekballo*, translated into English as *sent* and *send out*, respectively; actually have totally different meanings. The first word, *apostello* − from which *apostle* is derived − means 'to send forth, to send in service or with a commission'. It is to be sent out officially as a messenger with authority. The second word *ekballo* means 'to cast out'.[2]

Jesus intended to send the disciples into the world and for them to go voluntarily, once they were blessed with all spiritual blessings.

When this method does not work, Jesus has another method of mobilization – casting out workers. When 'the harvest is plentiful, but the workers are few' (Luke 10:2$_a$ NIV) God uses the second means to bless other nations. In the Old Testament, Daniel, Shadrach, Meshach, Abednego and others were in exile to be His lights to the world.

The Beginning of Mission in the Early Church: No Excuse Even in a Setting of Poverty and Pressure

In the book of Acts, gospel author Luke described an incredible setting for mission in church history. Consider the background of the time and circumstances when this literal mission mandate was given.

It was a dark period in Israel's history. Nebuchadnezzar, king of Babylon, had overrun Judea and captured Jerusalem in 597 BC, ending the independence of the Jewish state.[3] Almost 400 years had passed since Ptolemy invaded the land and captured Jerusalem in 320 BC. Israel had been largely under foreign rule for four centuries. The past 100 years of Roman colonialism proved to be a time of turmoil for the people of Israel as circumstances changed under different Roman leaders.[4] If you come from a nation with a history of colonialism, you can understand the situation. People lived under economic pressure with social unrest and no political freedom. In addition, the early church was very small in number (Acts 1:12-14). They had no church building for regular worship service.

It was quite understandable that in those circumstances the disciples asked Jesus to restore the glory of the Kingdom of Israel. (Acts 1:6). But God's concern is not always the same as our fleshly human concern. While the disciples' concern and prayer was for freedom and independence, Jesus said that 'It is not for you to know the times or dates the Father has set by His own authority' (Acts 1:7 NIV). It is not because He did not hear their prayers. In fact, God gave them independence more than 1900 years after the disciples' prayer (1947).

Jesus with one word 'but' turned the conversation to an issue far more important than political independence and economic restoration: the task of God's mission, known as the Great Commission. 'But you will receive power when the Holy Spirit comes on you; and you will be my witnesses in Jerusalem, and in all Judea and Samaria, and to the ends of the earth' (Acts 1:8 NIV). The word *witness* speaks of more than being a person who bears witness and testimony.[5] It is not merely about talking and oral testimony in a church meeting. A witness is a presence in the world as God's agent and evidence of His deeds. A witness of him involves our whole existence.

Jesus' statement regarded not circumstances but only the condition: 'when the Holy Spirit comes on you' (Acts 1:8 NIV). No other conditions were required to do His will. Humanly speaking, the church had limitations; it was poor, small in number, and not materially wealthy. Jesus told His disciples that, when the Holy Spirit came on them, they would be his witnesses in Jerusalem, *and* in all Judea *and* Samaria *and* to the end of the earth. This did not mean that the witness goes to the next level of geographical distance upon completion of the previous level. The word *kai* (translated 'and') means '*at once*'. The task of world mission must be carried on *at once* to the end of the earth.

A wrong concept exists in many places in the world that the task of world mission will only be carried out when their own 'Jerusalem' has been reached. Therefore, cross-cultural missions is often slow in beginning if not stuck, because the church never sees that their Jerusalem is maintained well enough for them to take a step of faith beyond their culture.

Other Excuses that Ignore the Great Commission

From Acts 1, the apostles' mission began; they did not wait until the church grew big and wealthy. When the Holy Spirit descended (Acts 2), Peter and the apostles began their powerful ministry that resulted in 3,000 believers added to his kingdom (Acts 2:41). The number of believers rapidly increased. The demand for workers and ministry also rose. Many things needed to be done to maintain and take care of the congregation. It was understandable that the word of Jesus in Acts 1:8 had been easily ignored; however, God never changed his mandate to be his witnesses to the end of the earth. In Matthew

28:19 Jesus says, 'Go…teach *panta ta ethne'* (all nations). This mandate is for *all* nations, not only for *some* or *several nations*. Believers should not be satisfied with reaching only the nation, culture and community they belong to and feel comfortable in. It is a clear imperative that the Gospel must be preached to the uttermost parts.

God is very serious with mission. When *apostello* ways (to be sent in a good manner) does not work, He still can use the *ekballo* way (to be cast out/ kicked out).

Acts 8 reports a great persecution against God's people. Except for the apostles, they were spread out as refugees throughout all of Judea and Samaria (Acts 8:1$_b$). Why did God not protect His people and avoid tragedy? Was He cruel to let this happen to His people? Was He not the same God who promised He had 'plans to prosper you and not to harm you, plans to give you hope and a future' (Jer. 29:11 NIV)?

In His sovereignty, God allowed persecution so that the believers would carry out his mandate. Persecution kept the believers from a daily routine full of busyness and maintaining those who already knew Jesus.

The believers were *scattered* (this word *diaspora* was used by the farmer who planted seeds) to all the places mentioned in Acts 1:8. Instead of falling deep into self-pity because of persecution and suffering, the believers preached the gospel – the good news. This could only happen when they were not focused on their problem. Instead, the early believers saw the bigger picture of God's plan and goodness despite pressure and difficulty. The joy of salvation was the strength that they preached and spread to people in the places where they were scattered. Luke reported the result in Acts 8:8 that 'there was a great joy in that city'.

Mission in the early church did not flow out of economic and social stability, but was based on the Word of God and the anointing of the Holy Spirit. It started with Jesus' words to a small group of believers living under pressure and without a church building.

Lessons We Learned

It is time for Christians in developing countries to change the ethos of *mission* and *missionary*. Even though more and more missionaries are sent out from developing countries, there is still a wrong ethos that *mission* is a word that only applies to western Christians.

Yet God is consistent with His plan for this world and the way he uses the church to carry his plan of salvation to the nations. The Lord Jesus said, 'And this gospel of the kingdom will be preached in the whole world as a testimony to all nations, and then the end will come' (Matt. 24:14 NIV). Understanding and obedience to his Word is the most important qualification in carrying out his mandate.

An Indonesian Example

The gospel first reached the Indonesian islands through Nestorian missionaries in the seventh century. Today's Indonesian churches are the fruit of a long process of gospel ministries following the arrival of the Portuguese in the sixteenth century. The Dutch who came in the seventeenth century introduced the Protestant faith.

Through a long history, after lingering monetary crises starting in 1997, deepening restlessness, disappointment and frustration are growing in the hearts of many people. It is God's *kairos* (proper time) for an opening to the Gospel. With escalating persecution in recent years, Indonesian Christians are experiencing greater unity in areas such as prayer movements. The sweetness of Christian *koinonia* is experienced among churches, especially in times and places of suffering. The encouraging result of this movement towards unity leads to synergies in different aspects of Christian ministries, especially in mission. Reaching unreached people groups in Indonesia and reaching beyond cultural borders is also happening.

The other side of persecution and suffering can be judgment! Purification must begin at the house of God (1 Pet. 4:17) and can serve as God's reminder, emphasizing the stronger meaning of sending out − *ekballo* − his people for mission.

Advantages of Missionaries from Developing Countries

I know what it is to be in need, and I know what it is to have plenty. I have learned the secret of being content in any and every situation,

whether well fed or hungry, whether living in plenty or in want. I can
do everything through him who gives me strength (Phil. 4:12,13 NIV).

When Jesus was on earth as a man, He identified Himself with the
people to whom He ministered (Phil. 2:2–10). Careful reading of
the four gospels tells us that most of the time, Jesus came to the
poor and despised, while the rich came to Him. We need to identify ourselves with the people we minister to before our message
will be accepted.

Simple lifestyle

Many people in developing countries are used to seeing and living
in poverty and under pressure. This leads to a simple lifestyle which
provides the ability to live with minimum facilities. Living conditions in mission fields are often different from those back home.
Living with the unreached means identifying with them, and most
unreached people today are poor. When accustomed to living in a
simple community, it is easier to understand the mindset of people
we serve. It is easier to live as they live without viewing it as a 'great
sacrifice'. It is easier to swallow their food and live with it. It is easier to reach out and mingle with them without fear of dirt and
suspected diseases; therefore, it is easier to identify with them. A girl
in an Indonesian village who has only one doll is very content; her
doll is her favorite toy. A girl from a big city who has many toys
becomes discontent and always wants more.

Complexity of language and culture

People raised in the developing world are accustomed to direct
encounters with different languages and cultures. Transitioning to
a new culture will not be too difficult an adjustment. With the
addition of formal training, they will more easily come alongside
the indigenous.

Contact with different religions and beliefs

Growing up in a multi-religious community provides a different
perspective and practical experience when meeting people who

hold other beliefs. It is not just paper knowledge but practical experience, learned from living together in community with people of other religions. Attitudes toward those of different beliefs are different when this already forms one's life experience.

Expectation from people we serve

One danger on the mission field is that people look up to missionaries as rich people. We come and live in better conditions than the locals. This assumption will be greater upon knowing that we come from a so-called 'rich' country. When people know we come from a developing country, they will stop expecting money from us. We are the same as they; we bring ourselves and that is all that we have.

Dependent on God

By nature, when we are in need we will be more dependent on God than when we are in plenty. While rich people acquire wealth with ease, it requires greater faith and miracles for the poor to obtain similar resources.

Disadvantages

None of this implies that missionaries from developing countries are better than westerners. The purpose of this article is to encourage Christians from developing countries – who live in a setting of poverty and pressure – that mission not only belongs to the West but is also theirs. Yet disadvantages also exist for missionaries from developing countries.

Feelings of inferiority

The background of colonialism, the power of money, and backward civilization have created an inferiority complex for people from the developing world. They view the West as superior in all aspects. Feelings of inferiority lead to the mentality 'I need help' and 'I cannot do it' – a mindset that mission is not for them.

Economic support

The Bible is clear that money is not the primary prerequisite for mission. But the reality of the need for financial support becomes a major reason why many cannot be sent out from developing countries, even though many are fully supported by Christians within their own country.

Things to Do

When God asks us to do something, he knows that we can do it. He never asks something from us which he has not given to us. Mission is the heart of God. He commanded every believer to do it. It requires creativity in communicating the vision and raising support and God's wisdom to make it happen.

Think beyond the box

Some people find it easier 'thinking outside the box' because they can see beyond their borders. It is more difficult for those to whom the box is their security. One must escape the box of narrow thinking to see the global reality and need for mission. We need God's eyes to see beyond the box – beyond capacity and ability – in the power of his Name.

Help from the stronger brother

The stronger brother needs to help the weaker, be it in knowledge, self-esteem or financial resources. Genuine help means to see long-term results which do not create dependency (mission impe-rialism) but rather a mutual *interdependency*. The help which weaker brothers and sisters need is to understand their capacity and to grow in maturity in fulfilling God's purpose for this world.

> For we are God's workmanship, created in Christ Jesus to do good works, which God prepared in advance for us to do (Eph. 2:10 NIV).

Bagus Surjantoro joined OM's ship Logos *in 1986. In1991 he became the national director of OM Indonesia, serving as well in a pastoral role and as a member of the Indonesia National Research Network. At the time of writing Bagus was on assignment to the leadership team of OM's ship* Logos II. *He and his wife, Delores, have two daughters and a son.*

1 Ralph D. Winter, 'The Kingdom Strikes Back' in R. Winter and S. Hawthorne (eds) *Perspectives on The World Christian Movement* (Pasadena: William Carey Library, 1999[3]), pp. 195-213

2 W.E. Vine., *The Expanded Vine's Expository Dictionary of New Testament Words* (Minneapolis: Bethany, 1984), pp. 1015-16

3 Merill C. Tenney, *New Testament Survey* (Grand Rapids: Eerdmans, 1985) p. 19

4 Tenney, pp. 25-36

5 Vine, p.1237

The Place of Networks in World Evangelization

A South African Perspective

Peter Tarantal

> *A missions mobilizer is a Christian who not only wants to get involved in evangelism and missions work but who wants to get other people involved as well.*
>
> George Verwer

One goal of the AD 2000 and Beyond Movement was, 'a church for every people and the gospel for every person by the year 2000'. One strategy employed to achieve this was the formation of tracks drawing together those interested in missions mobilization, training, worship, women's issues, and other interests.

During the early 1990s mission organizations and church leaders began an initiative called *Love Southern Africa* (LSA) – the South African chapter of the AD 2000 movement whose primary goal was to accomplish the larger movement's goal within South Africa. One strategy was an annual conference run initially by a mission organization to be later taken over by local churches. The conferences were intended not only to inspire South Africans for world missions but also to give them practical exposure by organizing short-term outreaches throughout the sub-continent. In addition to plenary sessions, participants were encouraged to meet in various tracks along the lines of the international movement.

In 1993 the first Love Southern Africa was held in Wellington (near Cape Town), organized by Operation Mobilisation South Africa. Approximately 1,400 participants from all over the country were enthused for world evangelization through speakers such as Operation Mobilisation's George Verwer and Panay Baba, director of Nigeria's Evangelical Missionary Society of West Africa. For the fraternity in South Africa, this was the beginning of tracks, eventually known as 'networks' defined by the Oxford English Dictionary simply as 'a group of interconnected people'.

In 1995 the Evangelical Fellowship of South Africa (EFSA) and The Concerned Evangelicals, together with other groupings which were not part of either of these bodies, formed The Evangelical Alliance of South Africa (TEASA). Up to this point EFSA represented mainly white Christian groupings and The Concerned Evangelicals mainly black groupings. TEASA became the South African chapter of World Evangelical Alliance (WEA). The missions arm of TEASA was known as the Missions Commission which had as its focus mobilizing for world missions churches affiliated to TEASA. Towards the end of the 1990s as the mandate of LSA was ending, the leaders of LSA and TEASA came together to pray for a new strategy of missions mobilization in South Africa. There was broad agreement that these two bodies should combine their efforts in an initiative called WENSA (World Evangelization Network of South Africa). The main purpose of WENSA was to empower and encourage existing networks to be part of fulfilling the Great Commission.

The chequered history of South Africa, influenced by the apartheid policies of the previous government, left its mark on the endeavours of world evangelization as well. People from various cultural backgrounds were not used to meeting together. Not only did the laws of segregation keep people apart culturally, but there was also a strong sense of denominationalism in the country. The networks sought to cross both denominational and racial barriers. To help make them more successful, I researched a number of these networks and present here some of my findings.[1]

1. Aims & Objectives

All the networks in the study regarded as their main goal to contribute towards the vision of Habakkuk 2:14, 'For the earth will be filled with the knowledge of the glory of the Lord, as the waters cover the sea.'

One positive trend in the last few years has been a greater Kingdom vision that developed between leaders across a wide spectrum of South African society which resulted in a willingness to work together. Most network leaders valued the opportunity to share resources and experiences. Other aims were the assembling of like-minded people to foster and encourage fellowship, and to help network members who were struggling in practical ways, such as training and sharing of ideas. Another goal was to encourage one another towards adopting a code of best practice.

2. How Networks Contribute Towards The Great Commission

The *Prayer Network*'s main goal is the mobilizing of 200,000 intercessors to pray for revival and world evangelization. At the beginning of May 2002, an initiative called *Turn the Tide*, co-ordinated by Walk Thru The Bible, with Bruce Wilkinson as main speaker, held a conference in Johannesburg. This presented an opportunity for the prayer network to link with churches and bodies across southern Africa via 300 satellite sites in prayer. The Concert of Prayer organized by the prayer network on a Sunday evening and attended by hundreds resulted in prayer not only for the continent but also for the nations. A special feature was six young people from the OM ship *Doulos* representing six different countries, sharing prayer requests for their countries. Africans, who can sometimes tend to be very inwardly-focused, became part of praying for the nations. A number communicated afterwards the impact such an event had on their own thinking regarding the world.

The *Training Network*'s main goal was the preparation of God's people to take their rightful place within world evangelization.

The *Poor and Needy Network*'s goal was caring for the poor of the world and brining the needs of the world to the attention of the church.

The *Missions Mobilisers Network*'s goal is to mobilize a new generation of missionaries. Through various meetings it has already seen a significant decrease in duplication and a spirit of competition.

At GCOWE '95 (Global Consultation on World Evangelization) in Seoul, South Korea, Judy Mbugua addressed the leaders of Africa represented at that conference from the passage Luke 19:28–34. Her theme was 'The Men of Africa should Release the Donkeys'. Her challenge was to the leaders of the church – on a continent where women are often viewed in subservient ways and have been undervalued – to allow women their rightful place. She spoke at great lengths of the worth of women and their contribution. Judy, who hails from Kenya, is the international leader of the Pan African Christian Women's Alliance (PACWA).

The South African version of PACWA is the vehicle for the mobilization of women's networks. It is encouraging to note an increase in the mobilization of women to pray for the least-reached peoples of the world. They are very involved in training women in prayer and evangelism. The leaders' vision is to empower South African women by teaching them practical skills such as knitting and sewing. Leadership development courses are also conducted on a regular basis.

3. Benefits of Networks

There is a greater synergy between participants in various networks. One leader described it as 'encouraging one another in gaining a greater enthusiasm for our collective work'. There is cross-pollination of ideas. A main building block of networks is solid relationships that are formed in the process, described as 'real and meaningful'. Participants receive mutual encouragement, share ideas and learn from one another. The leader of the training network has seen a greater increase in experts in one field being given opportunities to share with institutions that do not have necessary resources. One participant described it as 'being kept sharp and on the cutting edge by the interaction with others of that particular network'. We have already seen an increased sharing of platforms whereby people are no longer suspicious of others. Cultural, racial and denominational barriers are being broken down.

4. Constraints Faced by the Networks

The largest constraint often seemed to be financial. Because networks are nationwide, people have to travel great distances to meet.
Another is that network members seem to have full programmes
themselves and it is very difficult to work around everyone's diary
to get all participants together.

Leaders of networks would like to see an infrastructure that
would service the networks better. By their nature the networks
are co-ordinated on a part-time basis by leaders with other significant responsibilities with their own organizations or churches.
Ensuring participation by people of the previously disadvantaged
communities is still proving to be a challenge. Some leaders in
these communities view with suspicion anything that they have
not been consulted on from the beginning. Of course, years of isolation also contributes towards this. The great news, however, is
that this attitude is changing quite rapidly.

5. Practical Examples of the Value of Networks

In 2001, Campus Crusade for Christ leaders shared with network
leaders their vision for an initiative called *Operation Sunrise Africa*
calling it their 50-50-50 vision: to evangelize 50 cities in Southern
and Eastern Africa in 50 days, reaching 50 million people –
commencing 1 July 2002. As the leaders shared their heart for
reaching the lost within the areas mentioned, there was great
excitement in the room. The main thought of everyone present
was, 'How can we work together to make this happen?'

While the leaders of Campus Crusade presented the initiative,
their attitude was that it was a project for the broader body of
Christ. Co-operation of the various networks was essential for
the project's success. It is great to see how the various networks
are responding. As part of the Mission Mobilisers Network,
Operation Mobilisation has mobilized hundreds of young people
in a short-term outreach with thirty churches to reach the city of
Durban with the gospel. Young people together with their youth
leaders and pastors are coming from all over the country. There is
a two-fold spin-off: not only will the gospel be preached to tens

of thousands, but this practical exposure to missions will have a great impact on the lives of participants. The broadcasters' network also planned to saturate the sub-continent with evangelistic radio programmes.

Yula Franke, a pastor's wife and mother of three, grew up in Cape Town. Her story illustrates in a personal way the impact of networks.

Esme Bowers, leader of PACWA–South Africa, tried to involve Yula in their network. Despite numerous invitations, she was not interested but chose to watch from a distance. She had suspicions regarding the effectiveness of such networks. Her view was that often people in these networks talked a lot but very little happened 'on the ground'. Her interest was aroused, however, when she saw women from the network going into poorer communities and getting their hands dirty. They were getting women leaders in the communities involved in community projects. They were also teaching women how to be better mothers, giving them worth in a country where through racial and gender discrimination their worth was often eroded.

Having become quite inquisitive, when she was again invited by Esme to a conference in Botswana, she agreed to go. Yula wanted to see first-hand what PACWA was doing. Her attendance at the conference blew away many of her preconceptions. Several hundred women from fifty African countries attended this conference. Issues such as tribalism and the oppression of women were addressed. A special feature was how women can speak out against female circumcision on the continent of Africa. What impressed Yula was the willingness of women to 'call a spade a spade'. That cross-cultural exposure and experience had a big impact on Yula who, according to her own account, had tended to live in her own cocoon.

She came back to South Africa with a deep desire to become more involved in her own community and with a greater vision to empower others. Yula has now become involved with the activities of the PACWA network. She has also started attending Bible school in 2002 to better equip herself in ministering in local communities around Cape Town.

6. How a Co-ordinating Body Like WENSA can Help

Most network leaders believe that WENSA, as a central co-ordinating body, can help broaden the scope of networks. WENSA creates opportunities for networks to share with one another. WENSA can provide a platform to share ideas, as well as research and information.

Conclusion

One of the positive developments within the South African missions scene during the past fifteen years is that many solid relationships have been built – especially among and across various racial and cultural groups. Especially encouraging for me is the greater degree of Kingdom vision which has recently taken root in South Africa. Networks of mission and church leaders and organizations are playing a meaningful role not only in creating a mission awareness in South Africa but also by providing South Africans with practical ways of involvement in the Great Commission, moving us significantly beyond what we could accomplish on our own.

Peter Tarantal joined OM in 1987, planning to join OM's ship Logos. *Instead, he responded to the challenge of mobilizing the South African church, which, at that stage, had sent very few missionaries out from its shores. In 1995 Peer became the national director of OM South Africa. He is currently one of the co-ordinators of WENSA (World Evangelization Network of South Africa). He has also served*  *for five years as a national executive member of the Evangelical Alliance of South Africa. He and his wife Kathi have a son and a daughter.*

---

[1] Networks participating in the research were: The Pan African Christian Women's Alliance (PACWA), Mission Mobilisers Network (MMN), Caring for the Poor and Needy Resource Network

(CPNRN), South African Missions Training Forum (SAMTF), Association of Christian Broadcasters (ACB), and Jericho Walls International Prayer Network (previously NUPSA).

The Development of a Tentmaking Ethos in Operation Mobilisation

Howard Norrish

Whether you make shoes or microchips, God can use you.

George Verwer

After forty years of Operation Mobilisation history, we now have an ethos of holistic ministry – people finding their full potential in Jesus Christ so they can live with joy and dignity in transformed communities. I believe this ethos was grounded in our core values from the beginning of OM's ministry in the Muslim World. Tentmaking began in Turkey (1961), the Arab world (1962), Iran (1964) and Afghanistan (1968).

These countries were unevangelized because entry with a missionary visa was impossible. Entry was usually as a tourist. Many enrolled in university to learn the language. This gave a student visa and might enable a stay of several years. Long-termers became tentmakers – Christians working cross-culturally, recognized by the host culture as something other than a 'religious professional', yet in calling, commitment, motivation and training a 'missionary' in every way.

A commonly used scale defines three major forms of tentmaking:

1. Job-takers (T2) get employment and are paid according to a contract giving a residence visa.

2 Job-makers (T3 and T4) create employ
   validated by the government and gives a vis
   ment or a few people together starting a sma
   development work with an international or local N
3. Job-fakers set up a front for business or development ,
   no intention of working. They do the minimum for a
   There is no place in OM for job-fakers!

Whether the tentmaker is in development work (T4), the creation
of employment (T3) or in service to the community (T2) the goal
is always holistic ministry.

Turkey in the 1960s: the Pioneer Field in the Muslim World

Dale Rhoton and Roger Malstead were the first OMers to enter
Turkey in 1961. Roger was a student and Dale an English
teacher (T2). Their wives taught English. Most OMers in Turkey
in the 1960s were native speakers of English. Getting jobs as
TEFL teachers was relatively easy. OMers were tentmakers for
pragmatic reasons: people needed visas. But why was the transition so easy?

The 'Five Pillars of Tentmaking'

Five 'pillars' must be in place for tentmaking to be effective. These
are the biblical roots of a successful ministry. They enable the synthesis of work and witness. God, in his grace to us in OM, placed
all five pillars in our early thinking.

The lordship and sovereignty of Jesus Christ over all areas of our lives

No occupation stands outside his lordship. Everything we do is
equally worthy because the glory of God can be displayed in every
area of our lives. Teaching or research are as sacred as Bible study
and prayer. Development or business is as holy as evangelism and
Bible teaching. The daily work of a tentmaker is as sacred as leading a Bible study!

liligently and teaching effec-
oundations of being a biblical
'onald's *True Discipleship*.
d us think through the implica-
naking in OM was strengthened.
itegrates the dichotomy of the
red versus the secular.

ievers

The New ις.. is on the priesthood of all believers (Eph. 4). All have equal σιg.. y whatever their work. It is a sad fact that the 'mystery' of the clergy has frozen the laity in huge sections of the church over the centuries. If we are ever to evangelize the world, this frozen part of the church must be defrosted by a major infusion of redemptive energy. One of the curses of modern evangelicalism is that believers imitate, on a small scale and part-time, the work of a pastor, minister or evangelist. They consider their secular job spiritually meaningless and think really spiritual people are in full-time Christian work. This denies that the church is to glorify God before an unbelieving world by living as God intended us to live. The concept that the laity have a major role in missions and specifically in church planting was gifted to OM by God through our Brethren roots. This 'pillar' was built strongly in Turkey. Many workers there had Brethren roots.

Vocation and calling

In the Bible there is great emphasis on vocation − a calling from God to all children of covenant and grace to be his people, living faithfully and declaring his reign and kingdom (2 Tim.1:8–9; Rom.8:28–30; Eph.4:1).

In Western societies we divide our lives into roles: father, employee, citizen, football player, church member. Our 'vocation' is how we earn our living. Our spiritual calling is something completely different. Biblically this is a false dichotomy. Vocation and calling must be intentionally synthesized in a biblical worldview.

Tentmaking expresses the biblical truth that all believers are called to ministry and witness; none is exempt. The New

Testament emphasizes only one calling: the call to the service of Christ.

OM's emphasis in the 1960s was radical New Testament discipleship: all Christians everywhere should literally follow New Testament guidelines. There was also a specific calling to particular roles (bookkeeping, mechanics) or to certain places (India, Turkey, France). There was a downplaying of 'the missionary call'. We taught that all had a missionary call. We must mobilize the church. Awakening and envisioning is not enough. We must train people and keep them moving until they find their place in world evangelization.

This pillar makes the transition into tentmaking easy because it is based on a holistic view of Biblical teaching, not on dichotomized Western thinking. George Verwer taught this principle from the beginning and it is still a major theme in his preaching.

A Theology of work

Our view of work is determined by our view of the physical world. If that is seen as fundamentally evil we want nothing to do with it and our spirituality and favour with God will come from withdrawal to a monastic 'holy ground'. But Jesus taught that evil was *in* man (Mk. 7:20). Man is a spiritual being, put on earth to fulfil God's purposes. A primary purpose is to develop, protect and administer the God-given natural resources of the world. We demonstrate to unbelievers the nature and purpose of God by obedience to this command. The commission given to Adam was also given to Noah (Gen.9:1,2). David reaffirms it (e.g. Ps. 8:3–6).

As Christians we reject three common explanations for work: the judgement of God on our fallenness (his retaliation for our rebellion); survival (making a living); and as a place for evangelism.

Again it was Schaeffer's influence that laid into our ethos this pillar of the theology of work. One of the most innovative programmes in OM was Operation University (OU). OU sent people to L'Abri for a few months and then placed them in evangelism teams in universities across Europe. Schaeffer's influence in the Muslim world was considerable in teaching a worldview favourable to tentmaking. This happened because many OMers in universities in Turkey had been in OU.

We work for three reasons:

We fulfil ourselves as creative beings made in the image of God:
God is a creative worker, planning, designing, supervising (Gen.1).
He didn't rest until he had finished his work. He still sustains all
things by the word of his power (Heb.1:3). Jesus said, 'My Father
is always at his work to this very day and I too am working' (John
5:17 NIV).

Man in God's image is also a creative worker. Work makes us
more really human. But the climax of creation – the Sabbath –
sees man not working but resting for worship. Our humanness and
satisfaction in work must be in relationship not only with creation, but also with our Creator. Worship, not work, is the summit
of man's activity, but work is a vital part of being human. When
work is not linked to worship, its fallen character dominates so it
becomes a means to an end and a controlling power.

By work human beings serve the community:
Communities are interdependent. The priority of work is not
profit but service for the good of the community. When OM's ship
ministry started in 1970, everyone on board worked an eight-hour
day serving the ship's community. This was partly pragmatic, but it
reflects this pillar laid in OM in the 1960s.

By work we co-operate with God:
Partnership with God is the pinnacle of being human. The natural, social and spiritual worlds are the raw materials God has given
us. The Bible sees man in partnership with God – creating, con-
serving, cultivating and developing the full potential of the raw
material. This is our Great Commission. It finds fullest expression
in divine–human collaboration.

Schaeffer taught us to avoid two extremes:

- Work is a curse and the ultimate is a workless community
  where others provide for us.
- Work is an idol – the source of our meaning and identity.

To see work as a ministry is the fruit of faith. Like everything else,
work is meaningless apart from faith in God. It may be therapeutic

(since it was given before the Fall) but it must be redeemed from vanity (Eccl. 2:17-26).

Partly because of this, early OM teams supported themselves by bookselling. This was our *modus operandi*. Not only did we work for a living, we also established national workers in what we hoped were self-sustaining businesses – usually Christian bookshops. We tried to help them become self-supporting and not dependent on foreign funding – a good development principle.

Incarnational ministry

The final pillar of tentmaking is incarnational ministry. 'As the Father has sent me (into the world), so I am sending you (into the world)' (John 20:21 NIV). Incarnational ministry strives for deep identification with people in their culture and in their pain, frustration and troubles. It involves, as much as possible, becoming 'one of them'; coming 'in the form of a servant' – a selfless, sacrificial servant whose life is given for others. George taught us about living a *Calvary Road* life. The result was a commitment to a simple lifestyle. We wanted 'to sit where they sit' – to identify with people as Jesus identified with us. He worked for many years in T3 tentmaking.

Towards a synthesis of work and witness forged in the 1960s

These Biblical pillars provide the basis of tentmaking as a valid form of mission. The principles are broad enough to allow a diversity of models:

- The T3 model of tentmaking,
- The EBE model (Educational Book Exhibits, originally set up in Nepal as T3 in the late 1960s),
- The OM Ships Model – an extension of the EBE Model.

So tentmakers, by the empowerment of the Holy Spirit, can celebrate the fact that, by their work, they serve God and hasten the coming of His Kingdom. They know the Holy Spirit's help in their work as the tabernacle workers did in Exodus 31 and 35.

Operation Islam and the Book of Acts

In the 1960s OM's work in the Arab world, Turkey and Iran was called Operation Islam. Dale Rhoton's influence was immense. Dale and Elaine modelled how to do Muslim evangelism, how to think about culture, the importance of living above fear and other keys to effective ministry. Dale taught us biblical principles – especially Pauline missionary methods.

We consciously tried to follow Paul's example. Much teaching was on suffering, imprisonment and expulsion – seen as normative. Paul chose to work with his hands. This was his major strategy on all three missionary journeys (1 Cor. 9). Paul gave four reasons for working with his hands (as a tentmaker): credibility, identification, modelling and reproducibility.

Credibility

Paul's motives for preaching the gospel were above reproach. He worked with his hands to avoid putting 'an obstacle in the way of the gospel'. He wanted to be seen as making no profit from it. The believability of his message was crucial. He wanted to enhance this believability. In the Muslim world the credibility of OMers is a major issue. Missionary credibility is extremely low. Dale taught us always to ask ourselves, 'Is what I am doing or saying increasing the believability of the gospel or discrediting the Kingdom?' Many of us became tentmakers for this reason.

Identification

Paul adapted to the culture to win more people. To reach working people he became a working man. He took a menial job because most people are poor. This identification was not phony. Paul lived on his earnings. He worked hard. This was costly incarnational service.

Incarnational ministry is an 'issue' in missiology in the 21st century. This was something we learned through Dale's teaching and discussion on our teams about implementing these principles from Paul's life and ministry.

Modelling

Paul says, 'With toil and labour we worked night and day that we might not burden any of you and to give you an example to follow' (2 Thess. 3:8,9). Paul wanted to demonstrate living a life of holiness and godliness in the workplace. Not to work is not an option for the follower of Jesus, nor is withdrawal from the world. It is possible to live a hum-drum life, doing a menial job, and be filled with the Holy Spirit and called to an apostolic ministry. Paul shows how every believer can be an unpaid evangelist/church planter.

Modelling is crucial in disciple-making. Disciples are not made only through courses and a cognitive understanding of Christian truth. The key to discipling is replacing negative habits with godly virtues. This can only be done by modelling.

Fully-supported missionaries are only good models for full-time Christian workers! New believers in pioneer situations need tentmakers to model being a disciple of Jesus Christ. They need to see how to be a witness to Christ in the world they live in. It is vital that they stay within their communities and are not extracted from their cultural milieu.

Reproducibility

Paul's goal was to plant rapidly reproducing churches, resulting in an indigenous church planting movement – the only way whole people groups can be evangelized. Every newly formed church was involved in lay evangelism and church planting as soon as possible. They were self-supporting from the start and not dependent on funds, personnel or other resources from outside. The needs of these house fellowships were kept simple. They met in homes and everyone worked. Paul and his small team modelled being in fellowship together, being self-governing, being spiritually interdependent and being self-supporting and self-propagating.

By working among the poor, Paul reached the lower socio-economic classes who knew Greek and provincial languages of rural areas surrounding urban centres. In this way Paul reached whole provinces with the gospel. If Paul had gone to the upper classes he would only have reached the elite in the cities.

Paul did not stay long with the churches he planted. He equipped them to do evangelism and discipleship. Right away he made them aware of their missionary responsibility. He saw that this encouraged growth into spiritual maturity. These new believers could never say to Paul, 'You do the evangelism, we are far too busy working; you have more time than us.' Tentmakers do not encourage the clergy/laity split.

Does Paul's strategy work? Evidently it does! He spends a few months in some Galatian towns and the whole region is evangelized. He spends a short time in Philippi, Thessaloniki and Berea and all Macedonia is reached. He spends a year and a half in Corinth and all Achaia is reached with the Gospel. He spends three years in Ephesus and the whole Roman province of Asia hears the Gospel. In less than ten years four Roman provinces: Galatia, Macedonia, Achaia and Asia, are fully evangelized despite great difficulties and opposition.

By the power of the Holy Spirit, lay evangelists and reproducible church planting will give exponential church growth. Paul's evangelists were not missiological or theological experts from seminaries. They were poor, uneducated new believers from a pagan background. The difference was that they had a model – a pattern to follow!

In the New Testament, tentmaking is the preferred strategy for pioneering in 'creative access' countries. Scripture does not give us any other. Empirical data shows that tentmakers can start self-supporting, self-governing and self-reproducing churches equipped to reach local people with the gospel more rapidly than fully supported missionaries.

Developments in the 1970–80s in Turkey, Iran and the Arab World

There were two sorts of OMers in Turkey: those planning to stay two years and then move on, focused on reaching the masses – mainly through literature; and 'Turkey fanatics' who planned to spend a lifetime there in evangelism and church planting. These tentmakers had a long-term commitment. They hoped to see the start of a church-planting movement. They were involved in many activities: translation of the New Testament into modern Turkish; Bible correspondence courses; writing Christian books in Turkish; translating books into Turkish; radio programmes; discipling Muslim-background believers; starting churches; leadership development. They laid the foundations of the church in Turkey that others are building on.

In Iran the 'Turkey model' was followed closely until 1979 when Ayatollah Khomeini came to power and the OMers left. An American couple led a tentmaker team in Shiraz. They were influenced by tentmakers working in Iran and Afghanistan. In Afghanistan under Christy Wilson tentmaking was a well thought-through strategy.

OM began work in Afghanistan in 1968. In 1980 we pioneered OM's first T4 approach to tentmaking by setting up a development agency working among Afghan refugees. This was the forerunner of other OM-associated development agencies.

In 1979 Operation Tentmaker was launched. This was a training programme in London challenging students and people with professional skills to go to the Muslim world as tentmakers. This programme gave training in Islamics and Muslim evangelism including outreach to students in London. Not everyone on this programme was in OM. This initiative ended after two years.

In the Arab world, tentmaking was slower to develop as the focus was mainly on reaching the masses through literature evangelism. A leader moved from Turkey to Beirut and re-introduced tentmaking together with church planting as a strategy of OM.

In Turkey by 1988 there was growing religious freedom, making it possible to increase the number of workers from twenty to ninety-five. Many were tentmakers. In the Arab world, a tentmaking strategy with the goal of church planting helped raise numbers from fifty in the early 1980s to 250 in 2002.

In the 1990s, there was a growth of T4 with the start of several OM-rooted development agencies. More OMers explored the possibility of starting and maintaining business platforms (T3).

A major change in the 1980s came about through the arrival of tentmakers from the non-Western world – the 'new missionary-sending nations'. They brought with them many advantages.

- They are not seen as imperialists; with no history of colonialism, they arouse little suspicion,

- They know several languages and learn languages easily,
- Two-thirds world cultures are group-conscious rather than individualistic,
- They understand spiritual warfare; many come from backgrounds steeped in the 'spirit world',
- Most are from newly-planted churches and have a good understanding of church-planting,
- To Muslims they don't look 'Christian'. This arouses curiosity and makes evangelism easier.

We hope to see many more two-thirds world tentmakers in 21st century OM.

The Future Role of Tentmaking in OM

Tentmaking is the major way to reach the Muslim, Hindu and Buddhist worlds. The implication of this is that OM must put tentmaking at the heart of its ministry, thinking more theologically and missiologically. We must strengthen the Five Pillars of Tentmaking and the missiological principles of Pauline strategy. We have the needed structure in OM's Global Service as an entry door for tentmakers. We also need intentionality in the way we recruit and train tentmakers.

We hope to see improvements in T3 as small groups start up businesses together. Most of these OMers will probably come from the new missionary-sending nations. More OMers will be involved in development NGOs.

Tentmakers must co-ordinate with mass-media ministries. In OM there has always been a division between those reaching the masses and those 'making disciples' through church planting. The reality is that optimal effectiveness comes by focusing on both with good co-ordination.

Conclusions

Tentmaking is a missiological strategy to plant churches and evangelize whole regions. Helping churches to become self-propagating, self-supporting and self-governing will further this. Church planting movements start this way. It is the only New Testament strategy and is 'pillared' by Biblical principles.

In God's grace, many have looked to OM as a model for ministry. Tentmaking was at the heart of our early strategy. For OM to stay on the cutting edge as we go into the 21st century, our focus must be not only on recruiting and sending people, but on effectiveness on the field.

All current evidence shows that tentmakers plant 'reproduction-culture' churches more successfully than full-time Christian workers on missionary visas. These are the churches that will lead most easily to church-planting movements.

Dr. Howard Norrish joined OM in 1963. He met his wife Nora in 1965 on a team working among North African Arabs in the bidonvilles (shantytowns) of Paris. Between 1967 and 1983 Howard and Nora lived in Jordan, Lebanon and Saudi Arabia where Howard taught biochemistry in a university medical school. From 1983 to 1991 Howard was based in the Arab World Team administrative office of OM in Cyprus, serving as field leader from 1986. Since 1992 Howard and Nora have been part of the International Co-ordinating Team of OM in London with special focus on OM's work in the Muslim World. They have three adult children and three grandchildren.

Revolution of Love Rediscovered

A Plea for Holistic Work in the 21st Century

Bertil Engqvist

What I really find difficult is when people don't care.

George Verwer

'Do you have a suit?' George asked the Mexican pastor after the meeting. When the pastor answered in the negative, George immediately said 'I have plenty of clothes.'

'Here you are,' he said a bit later, passing a suit out through the car window as he drove away. The thankful pastor had no idea that this was the very suit that George had been wearing during the meeting.[1]

George Verwer was a revolutionary. He was one of those young people that had met the Risen Master who had touched their lives and turned their worldview upside down. Now they saw things as Christ saw them. It was no more a question of 'What can I get out of this?' but rather 'What can I do for you?' George lived what he taught. To love your neighbor meant not only to preach your faith, but live it out as well.

This incident in Mexico in 1957 was typical of George, but not of him alone. People deeply in love with the Lord Jesus Christ are changed. They do not see their possessions as their own, but as common belongings. The Church is a different kind of community where caring for others is its passion. This is the true revolution of love. What is more, as Dr. Francis Schaeffer pointed out, 'God has given the mandate to the world to judge the Church by their love for one another.'

> Everyone was filled with awe, and many wonders and miraculous signs were done by the apostles. All the believers were together and had everything in common. Selling their possessions and goods, they gave to anyone as he had need (Acts 2:43-45 NIV).

The ideal would be that all believers live such a holistic lifestyle. However, the Church has experienced a dichotomy between verbal proclamation and practical demonstration of God's love. A theological separation of spirit and body has relegated compassionate ministry to those for whom the infallibility of the word of God is of less concern. For George, holistic ministry was never a theological issue; he simply saw a brother in need. The natural response coming from a relationship with the living loving God is to help a person in need. Good fruit comes from a good tree (Matt.7:16-20).

Visible Proof of the Invisible

Apart from verbal communication, faith always expresses itself in some physical manifestation. Words might express faith but are weighed by actions taken. Christ himself implied that although one may not believe his words, one ought to believe because of what he did. Actions of love might be the strongest power encounter with forces of darkness or indifference.

James, who must have seen the early Christians in action, spotted the dilemma. Words could be cheap even if the value of their content was great. Therefore words could be difficult to believe. He sees the problem of a statement of faith without practical implications.

> What good is it, my brothers, if a man claims to have faith but has no deeds? Can such faith save him? Suppose a brother or sister is without clothes and daily food. If one of you says to him, 'Go, I wish you well; keep warm and well fed,' but does nothing about his physical

needs, what good is it? In the same way, faith by itself, if it is not accompanied by action, is dead. But someone will say, 'You have faith; I have deeds.' Show me your faith without deeds, and I will show you my faith by what I do. . . . You foolish man, do you want evidence that faith without deeds is useless? . . . [A] person is justified by what he does and not by faith alone. . . . As the body without the spirit is dead, so faith without deeds is dead (James 2:14-18,20,24,26 NIV).

Faith by nature is an active demonstration that the Kingdom of God has come among men. God has particularly chosen to make himself known through those who have been touched by his love. It means that the world with its limited understanding of destiny, or self-worth, or purpose would see and hear that God intimately cares for them − through the people of God. Thus Jesus' command to 'let your light shine before men, that they may see your good deeds and praise your Father in heaven' (Matt. 5:16 NIV).

God's love and care have never been solely verbal expression. The chosen people saw God's mighty hand rescuing them over and over again. He sent the written law, dynamic prophets and bold evangelists, but he always moved in the physical world. His words and actions go together. God said − and it was. He spoke and things happened. Even if He wouldn't speak he would still keep his creation and care even for the sparrow. God created out of love, and he upholds his creation through love. The ultimate price tag of his love is seen at the wooden cross − not only the mere thought of a cross.

For God was pleased to have all his fullness dwell in him, and through him to reconcile to himself all things, whether things on earth or things in heaven, by making peace through his blood, shed on the cross. Once you were alienated from God and were enemies in your minds because of your evil behavior. But now he has reconciled you by Christ's physical body through death to present you holy in his sight, without blemish and free from accusation (Col.1:19-22 NIV).

Love's Value has a Cost

God does not exclude his Church from hardships in the world but leads them through. In suffering and through difficulties we meet the Man of Sorrows and learn to experience and express the nature of the living God. Matthew 24 and 25 deal with the responsibility of the Church towards a world in massive suffering – which is nothing less than a strategy for world mission! How do we respond to earthquakes, famines, persecutions, wars, and so on? Christ states 'I was a stranger, hungry, thirsty, sick, in prison, naked…' The Scriptures imply that these humanitarian actions of response are done unto him regardless of their size. It is especially in those circumstances that the Church will show forth its brilliance. The calling is to a holistic ministry; therefore it is necessary for us to find ways of expressing God's unconditional love to suffering people.

A Palestinian beggar came regularly to us, trying to find food. She had lost her husband in the war of 1967. In the beginning she only wanted money. As we didn't have much ourselves, we gave her some of our children's clothes. She was very thankful. As time passed we started to exchange goods. 'Today I got enough tomatoes,' she would tell my wife. 'Do you have any eggs?' She also started to tell of her concerns for the children. We prayed with her. Toward the last days of our time in that country she only came for a cup of tea and prayer.

It can be gratifying to help people. One becomes important and needed, almost controlling the destiny of others. However, such motivation can be very selfish. But to work with human tragedies can also be disheartening. At times you do your best out of genuine compassion and all you receive in return are curses or hostility. It is humiliating to be on the receiving end as it seems to be a declaration of dependence. Although 'it is more blessed to give than to receive', it is not a simple matter. Benefactors can become so deeply identified with the needs and tragedies that they cannot live with the tension. As Tony Vaux says,

Failed idealism easily turns to bitterness. It may be helpful to recognize that these problems arise from deep contradictions in the notion of humanity – which is, in a sense, a selfish desire to assuage our own feelings of compassion for those in need as well as a desire to be altruistic. It involves a combination of personal emotions and societal norms…In other words, distress and suffering are the outcome of aid work, as well as its inspiration.[2]

The ministry of Operation Mercy is built on a conviction that God has commanded his Church not only to preach the Gospel but to love the peoples of this world unconditionally. We embrace the call of Francis of Assisi to 'Preach the Gospel at all times; use words when necessary.' We must be careful that we do not over-emphasize the Great Commission and forget 'the Great Compassion', as Dr. Peter Kuzmic expresses it. As we act with integrity, being what we are and doing what we say, people give us the right to speak. Charles Swindoll reminds us, 'I do not care how much you know until I know how much you care.'[3]

'If it had been two months ago, I would have torn it into pieces,' the young Kurd stated as he waved his newly received New Testament in the air. It was during the aftermath of the 1991 Gulf War. Thousands were driven up into the Turkish mountains. He had seen Christian love toward him and his people and that had changed everything.

The Lord has an unconditional, impartial love for all people. And the amazing thing is that God does not love because of our response. One day when Len, who worked in the Middle East, walked along the pavement with his close friend Hassan, Hassan suddenly stopped and asked sincerely, 'Len, would you love me even if I never became a Christian?'

The Logic and Moral Imperative of Compassion

The holistic approach gives special room for the gifting of God to his Church. There is a tendency to emphasize verbal gifts, e.g. preaching, teaching and prophesying while putting other gifts in a secondary category, e.g. contributing to the needs of others, show-ing mercy. God has gifted the Church with gifts of compassion to provide a platform for his truth and love on earth. The credibility of the Church therefore also depends on using the gifting God has given.

It is imperative that the Church in the 21st century involves itself in social actions if it is to remain relevant in society. Whatever the economic and social environment might be, we must partici-pate in meeting the needs of the world's marginalized people. In doing so, we regain the right to take an active part in shaping future society. A holistic approach to human needs brings hope in the midst of hopelessness. Genuine compassionate works of love pave the way for the establishment of the Kingdom anywhere, for as George Verwer has exhorted, 'No borders are closed for love.'

Holistic ministry aims to bring the whole of mankind into the freedom and dignity found in God's value of each individual, regardless of physical or mental capacity or racial, geographical or social background. It reaches out to help the needy and speak on behalf of the oppressed. It refuses to accept that a small percentage of the world is becoming richer and healthier through others' suffering. It rejects partiality, money or power of any kind as the basis for 'truth'.

Nobel Prize winner in Economic Science 1998, Amartya Sen states that the overarching purpose of development is the freedom of mankind. Present 'unfreedoms' hinder individual choice and stifle economic progress. The antithesis to these 'unfreedoms' is development.

> Development requires the removal of major sources of unfreedom: poverty as well as tyranny, poor economic opportunities as well as systematic social deprivation, neglect of public facilities as well as intolerance or overactivity of repressive states.[4]

Bertrand Russsell, a firm atheist, was once asked what he would do if, following his death, he were to encounter God after all. If asked by God why he did not believe, Russell said his reply would be 'Not enough evidence, God! Not enough evidence.'[5]

Certainly the appalling world in which we live does not – at least on the surface – look like one in which an all-powerful benevolence is having its way. It is hard to understand how a compassionate world order can include so many people afflicted by acute misery, persistent hunger and deprived and desperate lives, and why millions of innocent children die each year from lack of food, medical attention or social care. As Sen continued,

> The argument that God has reasons to want us to deal with these matters ourselves has had considerable intellectual support. As a nonreligious person, I am not in a position to assess the theological merits of this argument. But I can appreciate the force of the claim

that people themselves must have responsibility for the development and change of the world in which they live. One does not have to be either devout or nondevout to accept this basic connection. As people who live – in a broad sense – together, we cannot escape the thought that the terrible occurrences that we see around us are quintessentially our problems. They are our responsibility – whether or not they are also anyone else's.[6]

If anyone would be motivated to change this world and remove its 'unfreedoms' it ought to be the followers of Christ, who do not only have the reason but also the power to act through the Holy Spirit. It is time for a revolution against injustices and unrighteousness, against poverty and corruption, against selfishness and materialism, against child abuse and apathy toward HIV/AIDS victims, against pollution and destruction of the environment. We cannot stand as spectators any longer but should take charge and change this world. It is time to rediscover the revolution of love!

'It is only in the mysterious equation of love that any logical reason can be found.'[7]

'The only thing that counts is faith expressing itself through love.'[8]

Bertil Engqvist, born in Sweden in 1942, is an artist and art teacher by profession. Shortly after his conversion in the 1960s he and his family moved to the Middle East with Operation Mobilisation. He later became OM's Area Coordinator for that region, leading into oversight of OM ministries in the Caucasus and Central Asia until 2002. Bertil has been the International Director of Operation Mercy since its inception in 1991. Bertil and Gunnel have three adult sons and nine grandchildren.

---

[1] As recounted by Dale Rhoton in the foreword to George Verwer, *Out of the Comfort Zone*, (OM Publishing, Carlisle, England and Waynesboro, GA, USA: 2000) and online at {www.georgeverwer.com}.

[2] Tony Vaux, *The Selfish Altruist* (London: Earthscan, 2001), p. 173

[3] As quoted on a popularly circulated poster.

[4] Amartya Sen, *Development as Freedom* (New York: Oxford University Press, 1999), p. 282

[5] Emily Eakin, 'So God's Really in the Details?', *The New York Times*, May 11, 2002, downloaded from {http://www.nytimes.com /2002/05/11/arts/11GOD.html}, Oct. 25, 2002.

[6] Sen, *Development*, p. 282

[7] Attributed to John F. Nash on receiving the Nobel Prize for Economics, 1994, in 'A Beautfiful Mind', Ron Howard, director, Dreamworks 2001.

[8] Gal.5:6 NIV

Literature in Missions and Church Development

Gerry Davey

When I was a sixteen-year-old student, I received through the post a Gospel of John from a lady who believed God answers prayer and who believed in the power of the printed page. For two years I read that little booklet regularly until, at a Billy Graham evangelistic meeting in New York City, I was born again. The day following my conversion I began to evangelize with literature and personal testimony and I have continued to do so ever since.

George Verwer[1]

Christian literature is important to God and central to his self-revelation to mankind. The words *book* or *scroll* appear more than 180 times in thiry-four of the books of the Bible. And the phrase 'as it is written' or the command 'write these things' appears another 400 times. Books and writing are prominent in God's dealings with man – past, present and future.

In Genesis 5:1 we read 'This is the book of the generations of Adam' (NASB) and the emphasis is sustained through to the last chapter of Revelation where books are mentioned seven times.

Moses realized the importance of books in God's plan. Descending from Sinai and seeing the golden calf, he cried out to God, 'If you will not forgive the sins of your people once more, then blot me out of your book which you have written.'

The desire of the Lord Jesus is that his disciples' relationship with him be assured and stable and a source of rejoicing, so he commands in Luke 10:20, 'Rejoice.' Why? '…because your names are written in heaven.' He wants this relationship to be permanent, on a sure footing, and unchanging, so he uses writing as an appropriate medium that is fixed and reliable.

Books also feature prominently in God's future administration of his kingdom. Daniel 7 and Revelation 20 demonstrate the central role of books in God's final judgment. 'The dead were judged according to what they had done as recorded in the books.'

Both Weapon and Shield

One of the most striking pictures the Scriptures give of the Christian is that of a soldier. But in the fight against sin, Satan and self the soldier will not survive long without weapons. Literature has always been an indispensable item in the armoury of soldiers – Christian or secular – as it facilitates initiatives and advances.

'I would rather write a pamphlet than speak at twenty mass rallies,' was the rather startling assertion reputed to have been said by Vladimir Ilych Ulyanov (alias Lenin). And when the influence of his seventeen supporters in 1907 had mushroomed to control one-fifth of the world's population by 1990, his priority was confirmed, as literature had played a significant role in the growth of communism. The Soviet message was evil and corrupt but, partly because of the vigorous use of the weapon of literature, it was effective. How much more should the true, pure, liberating message of the Gospel motivate Christians to become skilled and disciplined in using this weapon!

Dr Donald Coggan, former Archbishop of Canterbury, wrote in his book *Convictions*,[2] 'We need a flood of literature which incorporates Christian insights and the Christian philosophy of life. To dedicate your life to this is to wield about the sharpest weapon for good and for God that any man or woman can handle.'

Literature not only facilitates spiritual offensives. Its role is often crucial in building up spiritual defences. Well-argued and charitably presented titles can play a vital role in helping believers detect, resist and refute false doctrines and the superstition which continually bombards the church in all generations.

Many Christians go through times of varying degrees of doubt and dryness concerning their faith, and well-written apologetics can help to stabilize and strengthen them in such periods.

Older believers are tempted to plateau out and fail to respond to opportunities or challenges in later life, but they can draw encouragement to press on from realistic biographies. God has probably used biographies more than any other single means to call missionaries into his service.

To have half a dozen books of encouragement with salient points already underlined can be a wonderful resource to fall back on in times of personal discouragement. A file of clippings from reports and periodicals on how God is working in the world today through literature can save us from depression when surrounded by problems and conflicts in our ministry.

The Reproductive Power of Writing

Throughout the history of the church, God has used books to permanently change individuals and nurture them into effective, productive ministry. John Wesley comes to mind with his heart that was 'strangely warmed' by the introduction to Luther's commentary on Romans. John Newton, captain of a slave ship, found faith and forgiveness in the middle of an Atlantic storm as he read *The Imitation of Christ* by Thomas à Kempis and went on to effective pastoral ministry and writing.

A tract by an unknown author led to the conversion of the Puritan Richard Baxter. He in turn wrote *The Saints' Everlasting Rest* (still in print today); this led to Phillip Doddridge becoming a believer. Amongst the hymns and books authored by Doddridge was the title *The Rise and Progress of Religion in the Soul.* This made a great impact on William Wilberforce who went on to be a great English social reformer. Wilberforce penned *Practical Christianity* which was instrumental in the conversion of Thomas Chalmers, founder of the Free Church of Scotland. A chain reaction from tract to the formation of a denomination in a future century – that is the power of Christian literature!

Another more recent chain reaction can be traced from George MacDonald's series of fine Christian fiction influencing C.S. Lewis.

Lewis, in turn, wrote more than forty titles. One of those titles, *Mere Christianity*, profoundly changed, amongst others, J.B. Phillips, J.I. Packer and Charles Colson, all of whom have contributed books that have significantly helped many thousands of people.

But we don't have to be an author to be effective in literature ministry. Actually, the bottleneck worldwide is in distribution.

George Verwer, founder of Operation Mobilisation and one of the greatest 'pushers' of Christian literature of modern times, has this testimony:

> When I was a sixteen-year-old student, I received through the post a Gospel of John from a lady who believed God answers prayer and who believed in the power of the printed page. For two years I read that little booklet regularly until, at a Billy Graham evangelistic meeting in New York City, I was born again. The day following my conversion I began to evangelize with literature and personal testimony and I have continued to do so ever since.

George is now sixty-five years old. Though he has spoken many thousands of times at meetings, large and small, throughout the world (and never without books to offer), he has never lost his enthusiasm, zeal and commitment for the distribution of Christian literature. He has himself authored several books. However, his heart remains in distribution, especially in languages other than English – languages read by many unreached peoples of the world. It has been a great joy and privilege for my wife and me to work with George in literature ministry for the past forty years in distribution in France, in Spain under Franco, as director for eighteen years of the ministry of Send the Light Inc in the UK, and in recent years developing indigenous Christian publishing houses in the former communist countries and working with George on a host of non-English-language-title projects! Through all these years George has never failed to challenge, help and encourage!

The Lessons of History

Significant books do not only record history; they help to shape history. Books provide a structure for communicating ideas; as thoughts are formed and stimulated wills embrace new priorities and motivations leading to changes in behaviour of individuals, communities and nations.

One of the most useful treatments of this subject is Klaus Bockmuel's booklet *Books – God's Tools in the History of Salvation.* First published in 1989, he establishes the crucial role played by books in the Reformation, the rise of Pietism and Methodism. He outlines the part played by literature in the fight for social reform in the UK during the 19th century simultaneously with the literature focus of William Carey, often called the father of modern missions. Bockmuel writes,

> Without the printing press the course of the German Reformation might have been different. Luther's own writings constitute a third of all German books printed in the first four decades of the 16th century. His 'Concerning Christian Liberty' was reprinted eighteen times in its first six years. Luther's translation of the New Testament cost a week's wages for a craftsman, but within two years of its 1521 publication there were fourteen authorized and sixty-six pirated reprints.

Books have influenced not only church history but the whole course of human history. 'All revolutions of the modern age were initiated by a campaign of printed materials of various kinds.' A war of ideas is first waged before a war on the battlefield. We have already mentioned Lenin, but who can measure the overwhelming influence and impact of Hitler's *Mein Kampf* and Chairman Mao's *Thoughts*? Billy Graham states quite categorically, 'Every momentous event in modern history, whether for good or evil, has been brought about through writing.' Words are powerful and books are powerful. As Christians who utilize literature, we must insist that our material is true to Scripture, relevant to culture and of enduring value.

The kind of seed we sow now will determine the kind of harvest we reap in five, ten or twenty years' time. If we publish superficial literature, we will reap superficial Christians. If our material is sloppy and not thoughtfully rigorous, its readers will tend to be careless and easy prey for cults and sects. If the appeal is mainly to the feelings and emotions, the recipients are likely to be unstable and poorly grounded. If there is an over-emphasis on the spectacular and dramatic, there will ultimately be a lot of people who end up hurt, confused and frustrated. Likewise, if the focus is exclusively on the intellect, we can expect believers who are argumentative, cold and lacking compassion. But if the seed we sow appeals to both heart and mind, we can more confidently pray for a harvest of Christians who are strong and warm, confident yet gracious and who know both what they believe and how to relevantly and compassionately share it with those around them.

Empowered to Greater Things

Words and ideas are not so easily distorted once written down. When it is important to have accurate records of communication, the usual and wise custom in many cultures is to insist on it being written down. 'Put it in writing so that it cannot be altered' (Dan. 6:8). We can easily be careless with words, but once we have to write we tend to become more careful. Good writing causes both the writer and the reader to think more precisely and deeply. Francis Bacon, a 16th-century English philosopher and politician, remarked 'Reading makes a full man, but writing an exact man.'

Literature maximizes and multiplies the Lord's gifts to his church. It enables people with a great ministry to have an even greater one. But, probably more importantly, it also enables ordinary believers to have an extra-ordinary ministry!

I am not an evangelist, but when I distribute the titles of Billy Graham or Luis Palau, I am doing the work of an evangelist and unleashing the spiritual impact of these great men of God.

I am not a motivator nor a missions mobilizer, but when I arrange foreign-language editions of George Verwer's titles I am extending the call for radical discipleship and involvement to multiplied thousands of believers.

I am not a Bible conference teacher, but when I get involved with the translation of Dr John Stott's commentaries into Russian, Bulgarian, Czech, Romanian, Estonian, etc. I am building up the church worldwide as I help to bring first-rate exposition and biblical understanding to thousands of Christians.

I have no gifts of literary composition nor the well-honed arguments of an apologist, but when I distribute the works of C.S. Lewis, I can influence literary and intellectual members of society.

In the same way, through literature I can be effective as a counselor, an admonisher, an encourager. The roles are endless.

In John 14:12, Jesus says, 'I tell you the truth, anyone who has faith in me will do what I have been doing. He will do even greater things than these because I am going to the Father' (NIV). Jesus' sending of his Spirit enables his children to do these 'even greater things'. Literature ministry is one way in which this is accomplished. How many people did Jesus reach when he was on the earth? Probably a few hundred thousand. But by his grace Operation Mobilisation has over the last forty-five years distributed around 1,000 million pieces of Christian literature. And OM is only one of hundreds of groups, not to mention hundreds of thousands of individuals, who have engaged in literature ministry.

A point sometimes overlooked is that literature can help all other kinds of ministry to be more effective. After forty years of involvement with books, I have come to the conclusion that there is no form of Christian ministry that cannot be strengthened, complemented, stimulated or enhanced by the use of relevant literature. Radio/TV/video, humanitarian relief and development, preaching, teaching, church planting, counseling, whatever – all can be given greater impact by sensitive use of appropriate literature. Literature given out before an event can create curiosity and arouse spiritual hunger; given out at the event it can consolidate the thrust of the message; given out after the event it can be an invaluable aid in follow-up.

Now More Than Ever – Books

Looking back on the last few decades, the vital place of Christian literature worldwide can be clearly perceived. According to *Operation World*, 'It is estimated that more than 50% of all conversions around the world are linked to Christian literature.'

But what of the future? Our hearts could fail us as we confront the daunting challenge of reaching the world for Christ. Let us take courage from the words of that great missionary to the Muslim world, Dr Samuel Zwemer, 'The printed page is indeed a missionary that can go anywhere and do so at minimum cost. It enters closed lands and reaches all strata of society. It does not grow weary. It needs no furlough. It lives longer than any missionary. It never gets ill. It penetrates through the mind to the heart and conscience. It has and is producing results everywhere. It has often lain dormant yet retained its life and bloomed years later.'

This was said long ago. We can hardly begin to comprehend the resources at our disposal in this century, as millions worldwide are able to download entire books from the Internet! What a day we live in for dispersing the written word!

> If he shall not lose his reward who gives a cup of cold water to his thirsty neighbours, what will not be the reward of those who by putting good books into the hands of their neighbours, open to them the fountain of eternal life?[3]
>
> (Thomas à Kempis)

Gerry Davey joined OM in 1963 after eight years in aeronautical engineering. For eighteen years he was Director of Send the Light (UK). He was a founder member, and chairman for ten years, of the British Christian Booksellers' Convention. Gerry has helped to establish indigenous Christian publishing houses in ten former communist countries and now serves as a publishing consultant. Gerry and Jean have four grown daughters. One daughter currently serves in Tajikistan and another in Nepal.

---

[1] From the introduction to *Literature Evangelism*.
[2] London, Hodder & Stoughton, 1975
[3] As quoted by Terry W. Glaspey in *A Passion for Books* (Eugene, OR: Harvest House Publishers, 1998), p. 97, cited on {www.community bible.org/library/quotes/quotes.htm}, 25 Sept., 2002.

A Checklist for Ongoing Renewal in Mission Organizations

Dave Hicks

Where two or three of the Lord's people are gathered together, sooner or later there will be a mess.

George Verwer[1]

The Bible and subsequent church history records the relentless slide of God's people from serving him to serving themselves, from the priority of seeking his kingdom and his righteousness to seeking other things first. I will never forget the words of Johan Van Dam, then OM Austria leader, in London when Cathy and I first joined Operation Mobilisation in 1967. 'Every year OM must be reborn in every team around the world.'

Ongoing renewal – rebirth if you will – does not occur automatically. Quite the opposite: without vigilance, vision and vigorous resistance to the natural forces of the status quo, mission organizations, like individuals, lose their first love. Over time they tend to lose focus and heart. They begin to look more to an idealized past than to how they can take new territory for God in the present and future.

In many ways OM began as a renewal movement not just drawing the church's attention to compassionate action on behalf of the most unreached but also to a vision of unfettered Christian living, calling believers to close the obedience gap between professed belief and actual practice. George Verwer has often expressed it as 'overcoming spiritual schizophrenia', as 'spiritual revolution' or 'hunger for reality'.

During more than three decades with OM in India, on the ship *Logos*, in North America and in countless international forums I discovered how challenging it is, personally and corporately, to experience and even desire ongoing renewal. For me the renewal process has come into even sharper focus recently when God surprised Cathy and me by calling us to another sister agency that is twelve years older than OM. Moving to Bethany Fellowship International has required me to freshly think through the dynamics of organizational renewal.

In this essay I highlight a checklist of critical factors which undergird ongoing renewal including: the essential role of one or more change agents, a growing vision of dependence on God, key relationships, forming or reforming the leadership team, clear vision, and the alignment of people and structures. I will reflect on each of these factors against the backdrop of the book of Nehemiah.

The Essential Role of One or More Change Agents

Others must have grieved over the reports of Nehemiah's brother and his companions when they returned to Persia from a disturbing visit to Jerusalem, but only Nehemiah heard in those reports the call of God to a history-altering course of action. By virtue of his obedient response, Nehemiah became the catalyst to revive the identity and dignity of the people of God. The initiative is always God's but he moves to renew, restore and rebuild through a person or a group of persons he burdens with his concern.

That burden attaches to a sense of destiny deep within the soul of the recipient. As Paul Billheimer has written, 'Because prayer is on-the-job training for the future rulers of the universe, when in His divine wisdom He decides on a course of action in the world He has created and governs, He seeks for a man upon whose heart he can lay that burden.'[2] God never answers a prayer which he has inspired until he finds a man to verbalize it, at least in his spirit.

- Checkpoint: Has God given you deep assurance that he has
  called and prepared you to be a catalyst to lead a group of
  God's people to the next level of his purpose? Are you resist-
  ing that call or embracing it?

A Growing Vision of Dependence on God

Nehemiah responded to the shocking news and an unfolding
sense of call by giving himself to prayer and fasting 'for some
days, day and night'. He contemplated what he should do in a
context of worshiping the 'God of heaven, the great and awesome God, who keeps his covenant of love with those who love
him and obey his commands' (Neh. 1:4,5). J.I. Packer says it well;
'God to Nehemiah was the sublimest, most permanent, most
pervasive, most intimate, most humbling, exalting and commanding of all realities.'[3] Personal and organizational renewal for
Christians begins with worship, wonder and intimacy with the
transcendent, creator, covenant-keeping God who stands by his
word and delights in his creatures. Prayer is the most eloquent
expression of our priorities. It confesses our total reliance upon
God, exercises our personal faith and demonstrates our love for
others.

The half nights and full nights and extended times of prayer
in OM have been a blessed battle. They were seldom easy, but
those sweet times of worship that often came in the early hours
of morning were precious. George Verwer's example of persist-
ence in prayer and worship are certainly one major facet of his
legacy.

We began our new responsibilities at Bethany by leading the
people of Bethany in *50 Days to Seek God's Face*. These times of
corporate connection with our Lord – primarily to worship and
listen to his voice – have become an annual emphasis on united
prayer and fasting. In a variety of ways the people of Bethany
sought him, listened and laid our future before him. A few months
later, as part of the new structure, we launched a Global
Intercession Department to optimize worship and intercession in
and for every part of Bethany Fellowship International to undergird Bethany's relationships, ministries and leadership.

Seven months after we came to Bethany God brought Jenny Mayhew, a former OMer and one of our board members, with several of her colleagues to 'plant a garden of worship and praise to the Lord in Bethany'. Five months before they had done a similar thing hidden away in a room in Taliban-controlled Kabul, Afghanistan. With us at Bethany for four days they joined twenty to thirty Bethany people in hour after hour of contemplative prayer and worship called *Ministering to Jesus*. Worship watch hours have multiplied since then supplementing many other prayer, worship and Bible study gatherings in Bethany's life.

Nehemiah was also a man of the word. His prayer in the first chapter makes constant reference to what God had promised. 'Remember the instruction you gave your servant Moses.' The physical rebuilding of the walls prepared the way for inner rebuilding of the identity of the people of God around the Law, the expression of God's moral character. Nehemiah's ambition was not simply to reconstruct the city's defenses but 'to revitalize a spiritual community'. Only a few days after the completion of the rebuilding project, hundreds of men, women and children gathered in Jerusalem for a New Year celebration in which God's written word played a central role. An outdoor public meeting was devoted entirely to the reading and interpretation of God's word.

Is renewal dependent only on prayer or the word? Of course not. It is the word, prayer *and* decisive action that counts. But how quickly prayer and worship get pushed aside. Nehemiah knew how to maintain the balance between prayer and action. When the coalition of enemies pressed in to stop his wall building, Nehemiah 'prayed and posted a guard night and day' to meet this threat. Nehemiah knew who God was and that this was God's work, not his. He kept putting the threats, challenges, discouragement and impossibilities of it all back on God. 'Our God will fight for us!' he confidently asserted.

- Checkpoint: Is dependence upon God and growing intimacy with him at the heart of your ministry? What course corrections should you make to move beyond lip service to build a stronger foundation in worship and prayer for ongoing renewal?

Relationships are Key

Relationships with God and each other are the only realities that will last for eternity. Satan is always attacking relationships and how easy it is to cooperate with him. Any organization more than a few months old knows how difficult it is to 'preserve the unity of the spirit in the bond of peace'. That is why Paul instructs us to 'make every effort' to maintain peaceful unity. Dealing with strained and broken relationships where many suns have set on suppressed wrath are the highest-priority issues if our ministries are to be renewed.

In God's kingdom, relationships are fundamental. Bringing change to a mission organization requires investing heavily in building relationships and trust with opinion makers and gate-keepers critical to accomplishing your mandate. Nehemiah made excellent use of his existing relational network and extended it quickly by focusing on the most important relationships that were critical for the success of his Jerusalem mission. With full integrity, he took advantage of the privileged relationship he enjoyed in Artaxerxes' court to secure needed permissions and resources. Strong bonds of camaraderie grew as the workers on the wall laboured together to achieve a common goal.

Especially in larger ministries, small groups are often needed to help people relate together in more than task. Cathy and I joined OM's first ship, the *Logos*, in the mid-seventies. We came at a time when the huge initial struggles of launching this new nautical ministry were mostly over. We were aboard only a short time when we noticed quite a number of isolated individuals in the midst of the crew of 135 people from thirty-five nations. To help nurture relationships, we launched a small group initiative called *Ship Families*. These structures gave everyone on board a group of six to ten with whom to bond, celebrate birthdays, and enjoy out-ings. Although the focus of these groups has taken different forms through the years, small groups on both OM ships have provided a place to grow kingdom relationships.

Probably the greatest change in my understanding of life and ministry through the years is the realization that our commission from God is not primarily a performance-oriented task to be accomplished, with relationships tagging along to help it go better.

Our commission is to nurture vibrant and growing relation. with the triune God and with each other. That relational realh. true Biblical community, then becomes the context in which a multitude of tasks can be accomplished.

Gilbert Bilezikian paints this picture of the power of true relational community:

> The making of community cannot be a side issue or an optional matter for Christians. It is as important to God as one's individual salvation. Without community, there is no Christianity. Perfect community is to be found at the intersection of the two segments of the cross, where those who are reconciled to God can be reconciled together. Community is central to God's purposes for humankind. . . Watch community take on the powers of hell; subdue the rulers, the authorities, and bring them bound and screaming for mercy under the transcendental, heaven-and-earth sovereignty of our Lord Jesus Christ.[4]

- Checkpoint: Are you investing in relationships with those closest to you: with your spouse, your children, and your coworkers? Relationship building takes time but it's worth it.

Forming or Reforming the Leadership Team

After the wall was built Nehemiah put his brother, Hanani, in charge of Jerusalem, not because of nepotism but because 'Hanani was a man of integrity and feared God more than most men do'. Nehemiah formed an important partnership with Ezra to restore the Law to its central place, which led the way for the Jewish remnant's covenant renewal.

To bring renewal to an organization that has been around awhile you must have the right leadership team. There may be members on the existing team who are looking more to the past than to the future. Some members may not be ready to invest the intensive effort needed to redevelop the organization. 'We have already done all that before,' you may hear them say. Other key persons may not be included on the current directional team. Indeed you may need to recruit them. *Do not start by setting a new vision and strategy. Instead, eople on the bus, the wrong people off the bus, and the right seats – and then figure out where to drive it!* That lictum from organizational consultant Jim Collins ss that is relationally complex, especially in a ____ mission environment.

When I came to Bethany, I struggled to clarify the vision for its future. After determining only the broadest strokes of vision I turned my focus to the overall leadership team that was too large to effectively lead the organization. I spent my first six months getting to know the leaders and selecting a much smaller group composed of four vice-presidents of major areas in which significant results were required if we were to accomplish our vision and purpose: Global Ministry Impact, Global Ministry Preparation, Global Intercession and Business/Operations. Once the new leadership team was formed, we developed other forums to include the former members in the communication and decision-making loop.

John P. Kotter lays out an eight-stage process of creating major organizational change. The second step of that process is 'Creating the Guiding Coalition: putting together a group with enough power, expertise and credibility to lead the change and getting the group to work together like a team.'[5]

Key people not on the ongoing leadership team may supplement the guiding coalition for limited periods of time. Once created, the senior leadership group needs to be developed as a functioning team. A process created by Leadership Catalyst International[6] provides smart tools for growing trust in leadership teams. Enhancing relationships of trust and environments of grace within the senior leadership team has profound trickle-down effects on the whole organization. This process puts the emphasis on building a relational community where 'people feel safe, they grow up, they trust each other, they live authentically, they celebrate each other, they laugh a lot [and, on top of it all] they produce better.'[7]

- Checkpoint: Do you have a leadership team or are you trying to go it alone? Do you have the right people on your team to change the direction of your organization? Do you have an effective way to build your team?

Clarifying Vision

Over time organizations tend to multiply their ministries, adding to their reach and complexity. As diversity increases, attention needs to be given to the elements that hold the organization together including common beliefs, purpose, values and vision of a preferred future. As these elements are rearticulated, what you should be doing becomes clearer. So does what you should stop doing.

A new ministry never begins without identifying a need to be met. Nehemiah's brother and friends clearly defined the problem to be solved: 'Those who survived the exile and are back in the province are in great trouble and disgrace. Jewish exiles are in great trouble and disgrace because of Jerusalem's broken-down walls and burned gates.' To rebuild the physical wall and to proclaim and obey the word of God in the life of the city became Nehemiah's purpose. The picture, vividly painted by Nehemiah for Artaxerxes and the Jews in and near Jerusalem, described a safe Jerusalem, defined and protected by rebuilt walls and gates.

When the walls were finished, Nehemiah empowered Ezra to rearticulate the vision of being God's people through understanding and applying the Law and renewing their covenant with God. When an organization develops new vision, it is essentially starting a new life cycle. If this vision is strong enough, it not only can reverse stagnation, but also can take the organization back to the growth cycle. Suddenly there is a new goal to aim for, and new people and programs spring up around this new direction.

- Checkpoint: Are your purpose, vision and values clearly and compellingly written? When was the last time you stopped doing something because it was not at the core of your purpose?

Alignment of People and Structures Around Vision

Nehemiah was a gifted manager. The grandest vision without the ability to align people, structures, materials and other resources around that vision is nothing but a pipe dream. Nehemiah brought the resources and the people together to fulfil the wall-building vision by deploying a willing work force of forty-three parties across the forty-two wall sections and gates.

Because Bethany is a cluster of ministries including a college of missions, a mission agency, an urban ministry, a printing company, a local church and a network of global mission partners, clarifying the central vision that unites us all has become a priority endeavour.

Our board of directors clarified our purpose about a year ago; their primary task is to hold us accountable to accomplish that purpose.

Our leadership team is continually working to achieve optimum alignment between various ministries, making sure the right people are in places best suited to their gifts and experience and that our structures minimize wasteful duplication of effort. But optimum alignment occurs only when the vision is clear and compelling. Achieving optimum alignment is often a painful process requiring heavy leadership investment in relationship building, enhancement of capacities and clarity of vision – which takes time and effort.

- Checkpoint: Is there a high degree of alignment between your organization's purpose and the purpose of individual people, teams and programs of your overall mission? If not, how can you begin to build greater alignment?

We have surveyed six critical ingredients that contribute to ongoing renewal in mission agencies: the essential role of one or more change agents, a growing vision of dependence on God, key relationships, forming or reforming the leadership team, clear vision, and the alignment of people and structures. In reality these components do not necessarily occur in any particular order. Spiritual disciplines and relationships with God and others are primary in any work of God. But vibrant spirituality must be combined with leadership vision, alignment to purpose and faith-filled action to renew the ministry and multiply its impact on the world.

When several and, at times, all of these and other dynamic elements are interacting simultaneously, ongoing renewal can be reality for any mission that will pay the price. When these steps are taken, as Johan Van Dam said so many years ago, every year Operation Mobilisation (and other mission organizations) must (and can) be reborn.

For Further Reading

William Bridges, *Managing Transitions: Making the Most of Change* (Reading: Perseus Books, 1991)
Raymond Brown, *The Message of Nehemiah* (Leicester: IVP, 1998)
Larry Crabb, *The Safest Place on Earth: Where People Connect and Are Forever Changed* (Nashville: Word Publishing, 1999)
J David Schmidt, *The Prospering Parachurch: Enlarging the Boundaries of God's Kingdom* (San Francisco: Jossey-Bass Publishers, 1998)
Marshall Shelley, *Renewing Your Church Through Vision and Planning: 30 Strategies to Transform Your Ministry* (Minneapolis: Bethany House Publishing, 1997)
Dan Southern, *Transitioning: Leading Your Church Through Change* (Grand Rapids: Zondervan, 1999)
John White, *Excellence in Leadership: The Pattern of Nehemiah* (Leicester: IVP, 1986)

Dave Hicks is President/CEO of Bethany Fellowship International in Minneapolis, Minnesota, USA. Dave and his wife, Cathy, joined OM India in 1967 where they served until 1974 when they joined OM's ship Logos. In 1980 they came ashore and joined OM USA where Dave served as US Director for ten years and as North American Area Coordinator from 1984 to 2000. Dave and Cathy have four children, three born in India and one in Kenya. They are proud grandparents of eight.

---

[1] *Out of the Comfort Zone*, p.xiii.
[2] Paul E. Billheimer, *Destined to Overcome: The Technique of Spiritual Warfare*, (Ft. Washington: CLC, 1982), p. 47
[3] J.I. Packer, *Passion for Faithfulness: Wisdom from the Book of Nehemiah* (Wheaton: Crossway Books, 2000), p. 88

[4] Gilbert Bilezikian, *Community 101, Reclaiming the Local Church as Community of Oneness* (Grand Rapids: Zondervan, 1997), pp. 35, 186

[5] John Kotter, *Leading Change* (Boston: Harvard Business School Press, 1996), p. 21. The eight stages are: establishing a sense of urgency, creating the guiding coalition, developing a vision and strategy, communicating the change vision, empowering broad-based action, generating short-term wins, consolidating gains and producing more change, anchoring new approaches in the culture.

[6] www.leadershipcataylst.org

[7] Bill Thrall, Bruce McNicol and Ken McElrath, *The Ascent of a Leader: How Ordinary Relationships Develop Extraordinary Character and Influence* (San Francisco: Jossey-Bass, 1999), p. 30

Cookbooks, Firemen, Jazz Musicians and Dairy Farmers

Strategy and Research for 21st Century Missions

David Greenlee

God is seeking men and women of reckless faith today...to be reckless in your faith does not mean to be unthinking, but the reverse – concentrated, single-minded in your concern that God should be glorified and souls won.

George Verwer

'Our teams have been working in the country for ten years,' the missions leader told me. 'We entered at a time of major political change but, now that the excitement is over, we really don't know what our purpose is.'

'40,000 come to Christ!' trumpeted the mission news service. Some months later, a colleague confirmed to me the great things that had happened, but was hard-pressed to name more than a handful who were incorporated in the churches.

'What do you think?' I asked George Verwer early in my OM career. 'I am going to the capital to sort out the immigration problems so that the ship *Doulos* can remain in this country for the planned ninety days. But I am also going with suitcase packed and a back-up plan to fly to the Bahamas to arrange on short notice a visit there. Is that a lack of faith?'

'Faith doesn't have just Plan A and Plan B,' George replied, 'it has Plans X, Y, and Z as well!'

Mission strategy is a complex thing! On the one hand, we must depend on God's Spirit to do the work. On the other hand, God has given us responsibility to carry out the Great Commission he has also given. How can we understand our situation and make the most of what God has invested in us?

Cookbooks and Firemen

In America we call her Betty Crocker. The Swiss call her Betty Bossi. Matronly women, these ladies adorn cookbooks on countless kitchen shelves. All you have to do – we are told – is to follow the simple instructions and, just as in Betty's illustrations, out of the oven will pop a magnificent cake, succulent roast, or tender Chinese vegetables.

Some approaches to missions are like this: take a few workers, mix in a seminar or evangelistic plan, stir with a prayer walk, and out pops a church!

I realize that no one is that simplistic, yet we must admit that many approaches to missions are 'cookbooks', especially those plans developed far from the field of service. Like my failed cakes and Chinese cooking, somehow the results don't look as good as Betty – or the textbook – wants me to think they should be!

In my cooking, I may take account of high altitude or that the ingredients in the country where I live are not the same as back home. In missions, I may adjust for cultural and other differences. But too often we forget the human factor: missionaries and those they reach don't always respond predictably. And there is also the 'God factor': God does things in surprising ways, and with surprising people.

I am all in favour of good cooking, and in missions I prefer good planning. Knowing the 'textbook approach' may be a good beginning. But in humility we need to remember that missions is not accomplished by simple recipes.

Another form of mission strategy is the 'fireman' approach. Firemen respond to emergencies with lots of energy, flashing lights and noisy sirens. It makes for a great lead story in a newspaper or on the evening news. Firemen are vital public servants. But they tend to rescue, not to repair or build. After the emergency, someone needs to clear the debris and try to get life back to normal.

So, too, in missions. Here I am not criticizing the vital, well-planned ministries of emergency relief and community development. Instead, I speak of the danger of being missionary firemen. Swayed by the latest fad, they rush in, cameras flashing, Internet connections streaming, simply because there is an opening or pressure to be engaged in 'training' or 'ministry to Muslims' or whatever else the current missions trend tells them they should be doing. And, of course, they *must* say that 'serving in partnership with the national church' is their practice.

Jazz Musicians

My preferred image of mission strategy is the jazz musician. Although never an accomplished musician, in university I did enjoy playing trumpet in a small stage band and learned to appreciate the skills of some truly great musicians.

Those men and women studied hard to learn the basics then developed skills that enabled them to make beautiful music. As they 'jammed' they knew more or less where they were headed – even if not sure how the music would develop to get them there. They took turns playing lead and back-up parts. Dissonance was turned into harmony by passing into a new key. Even while improvising the musicians knew, musically, where they were heading.

Central to all this was skilful leadership. The bandleader might not have learned to play all the instruments, but he knew his band and the music they were capable of producing. Sensing the spirit of the music, the leader delighted his audience whether rehearsing old melodies or creating new sounds to fit the setting.

The parallel to mission strategy is obvious. It is not enough to just 'go with the spirit' of things; we need to know the basics. Learning the language, knowing God's Word and other core skills cannot be overlooked. But we also need to be prepared to adapt to the fuzzy edges of reality, the unpredictable situations we will face. We do not dwell on discord, but turn pain into 'passing notes' which enrich the beauty of our lives and ministry. Listening to each other and following our Leader, we can truly make beautiful music.

Research that Leads to Change

Leadership theory can help us develop our approach to strategy. But how can we understand complex situations (reality) and modify our approach to meet the need?

When we speak of mission research, commonly we think of lists of unreached peoples and statistics on evangelization. *Operation World*, the Joshua Project, and the *World Christian Encyclopedia* have provided mission leaders and lay people alike with tremendous resources to understand the needs of the world. Demographic studies which inform us of AIDS infection rates, illiteracy, or other social trends may point to needs for Christian ministry. Maps, a key feature in many OM prayer meetings, help us visualize the needs.

The use of statistical and demographic tools in mission strategy is common and fairly well understood. We need more of this type of missions research. But missionary strategists need another tool to understand the impact of their own ministries and respond to changing situations. I refer to it as *applied evaluative research*. Let me illustrate with an example from OM Ships.

In 1986, the *Doulos* sailed along the West African coast. Evangelists reported over 3,000 decisions in Sierra Leone during a three-week visit. Hundreds were reported to profess faith in Christ in other countries of the region.

Four years later, as program director of our ship *Logos II*, I was concerned that we have an effective program in our upcoming West Africa tour. I asked those doing survey trips to discern what lasting impact there had been from the *Doulos* evangelism four to five years earlier. To my chagrin, they did not give me even a single report of an individual faithfully participating in a church who had come to faith through the *Doulos* ministry. I believe that some definitely did come to know Christ but, at least in those investigations, we did not find anyone living out their faith in the fellowship of the churches with which we were in touch.

To me, and to my colleagues, this was unacceptable and demanded changes in the way we went about evangelism. We placed far more emphasis on follow-up: establishing a workable system, training interested Christians from cooperating churches, and emphasizing repeated contact with any who had professed faith while the ship was still in port.

Rather than 3,000 professions of faith in one port, we may have had something like 3,000 in ten or twelve ports altogether. However, a year later we checked with the sponsoring committees of pastors and Christian leaders. In one port we heard of fifteen going on for the Lord, in another thirty and similar numbers in other countries.

What had made the difference? I can point to four items: (a) a Spirit-inspired concern led to (b) some basic evaluative research; (c) the results were looked at with missiological eyes and (d) those empowered to make change did so.

Daniel Rickett of Partners International wrote that evaluation is an ongoing process, not something just stuck onto the end. He believes that:

> Unless ministry leaders see evaluation as the feedback loop to orga-nizational learning that directly helps them to lead, they will never have time for it. The evaluation function needs to be redefined and reoriented...Perhaps in the days to come, more healthy 'learning organizations' will build evaluation into their normal organizational lives. And donors will no longer need to ask the wrong questions when insiders are already asking the 'right questions'.[1]

Rickett, like me, is not looking for a donor-driven 'bang for the buck' evaluation, merely asking if we met our goals. Instead, we need research that looks at the broader consequences of our min-istry, develops our understanding of the situation and, coupled with missiological reflection, leads to a more adequate Christian response.

Elsewhere I have written of some of the technical matters involved in applied evaluative research.[2] There, and in numerous books, ideas are developed regarding research methodology. Rather than repeating that somewhat technical discussion, I would like to point to six important issues in bringing applied evaluative research into greater emphasis in mission strategy.

First, applied evaluative research must be appreciated at all levels and required by senior leadership. The attitude of the director of one min-istry who has told me to 'ask the hard questions and don't pull any punches' has led to robust evaluation of that ministry and a sharp-ened focus for the future. When senior leaders own the research,

...s need not feel threatened; all can openly enter into the
as a better future is sought.

*ond, we need more emphasis on research that links missiology to
...ation.* More than merely a goals-oriented or economic
analysis, we need to ask how people are coming to faith, how
churches are growing, how leaders are being trained. The findings of such research projects will not be written in prescriptive
'how-to' manuals. Instead, recommendations may take the form
of probing questions, challenging readers to think, apply, respond
and change appropriately.

*Third, although such research should be owned by senior leaders, we
must ask where the heart of the research lies.* Long ago a senior
researcher from another organization advised me to base myself as
close to the field as possible, yet with good communications links.
His advice is valid. Top-down, headquarters-centered research is
seldom appreciated. Projects need to be firmly grounded in the
field and presented in a way which will help workers get on with
their tasks.

Fourth, it is not enough merely to speak of research. Whether field
workers or home office staff, missionaries need to learn how
research can benefit them. This type of research need not be something distant and academic; only a few will develop professional
research skills. Instead, in our training and in our setting of strategy, we need to emphasize more an evaluative mindset. Global
Mapping's *Breakthrough Training* {www.gmi.org} is an excellent
model, turning real-life concerns into bite-size pieces, and developing more a way of thinking than a technical skill.

*Fifth, we need to remember that this sort of research need not be heavy
on statistics and fill-in-the-blank surveys.* Instead, smaller groups and
ethnographic methods can yield very helpful results. A case study
of fifteen women who turned from Islam to Christ did not produce a definitive, global paper on how such women are coming to
faith. But it did raise significant issues and had the potential to help
some missionaries assess their impact and the nature of training
given to new workers.

*Finally, we must help our mission leaders publish only developments
which can be verified.* We should be especially careful when we refer
to the numbers we have evangelized, reached, or trained. God
frequently does spectacular things – but are the stories we report

typical or exceptional? Applied evaluative research can help us tell the difference and better assess the lasting results of our work. Healthy skepticism may help us avoid repeating fantastic stories that, despite how good they sound, do not represent the real situation.

In forming mission strategy, therefore, we need to know the basics – for which 'cookbooks' can be helpful. Critical situations at times will demand a 'fireman' approach but fads and image should never define our vision. The preferred model of strategy is of the jazz musician: working with a team, building on well-honed basic skills, responding to ever-changing situations to make beautiful music.

Finally, the Dairy Farmers

For centuries my Swiss wife's ancestors have done research. Dairy farmers from Adelboden, they would not have called themselves researchers, but as they observed weather patterns, measured milk production and noted subtle changes in their cheese they learned and then adapted their ways to achieve desired results.

Our nephews who enter farming today have more formal training than their forefathers but – perhaps more importantly – they have learned how to combine their own informal research with the findings of agricultural scientists to maximize yields while protecting the environment. They don't change their ways simply to follow a fad or a rumour from another country, and they disdain legalistic restrictions from bureaucrats who have forgotten the feel of the land. But they listen, they learn, they talk together, and – when the scientific claim matches their understanding of the situation – they apply new ideas.

If missionaries should be jazz musicians in terms of strategy, they should be dairy farmers regarding research. The analytical sense of the worker in the field should be coupled with those offering a specialized skill to increase understanding, suggest new ways forward, and maximize fruit.

Jazz musicians and dairy farmers. Mission recruiters may not have them at the top of their priority but, in 21st century missions, we need them to help us know where we are going and how we should get there.

Dr. David Greenlee is Operation Mobilisation's International Research Associate. Raised of missionary parents in Colombia, David joined OM during the 1977 Mexico Christmas outreach. After sixteen years serving with OM Ships and completing doctoral studies at Trinity Evangelical Divinity School he became field leader of OM's ministries in a 'creative access' region. David is a visiting faculty member of Tyndale Theological Seminary near Amsterdam and teaches in other settings around the world. David and his wife Vreni reside in Cyprus and have three teenage children.

---

[1] Daniel Rickett, 'Healthy organizations learn the benefits of appropriate ministry evaluation', GMI World, Spring 2001.

[2] *Making our Greatest Contribution: How Evaluative Research can help Field Ministries.* Presented at the Third Lausanne International Researchers Conference, 4–8 September, 2001, Chiang Mai, Thailand.

The Reach of Evangelism

Robert E. Coleman

It's so easy to lose the vision for souls... if you have no time to drop your important job and tell someone about Christ, then you are too busy.

George Verwer

An artist, seeking to depict on canvas the meaning of evangelism, painted a picture of a storm at sea. Black clouds filled the sky. Illumined by a flash of lightning, a little boat was dashed against breakers and was disintegrating under the pounding of waves. Sailors were struggling in the swirling waters for survival, their anguished voices crying out for help. The only glimmer of hope was in the foreground where a large rock protruded out of the sea. And there clutching desperately with both hands was one lone seaman.

It was a moving scene. Looking at the painting, one could see in the tempest a symbol of humanity's hopeless condition. And, true to the Scriptures, the only way of salvation was 'the Rock of Ages, a shelter in the time of storm'.

But as the artist reflected upon his work, he realized that he had not accurately portrayed his subject. Seeing his error, he painted another scene similar to the first. There was the same storm: the black clouds, the flashing lightning, the angry waters. There was the same little boat crushed against the breakers, its crew vainly struggling in the waves. In the forefront was the same large rock and the same seaman holding on for salvation. But the artist made one change in the picture: the survivor was now holding on with one hand, and with the other, he was reaching down beneath the waves to lift up a sinking friend.

That is the picture of evangelism: that hand reaching down to rescue the lost. Until that hand is offered, there is no Gospel and no salvation.[1]

Good News in Christ

Evangelism offers salvation through Jesus Christ to perishing men and women. Nothing can be more relevant for mankind, both individually and corporately, is utterly 'dead in trespasses and sins' (Eph. 2:1), without any natural resource to save itself. To men dying in this despair, under the judgement of hell, learning that redemption has come is good news indeed. The word 'evangelize' literally means 'to bring good news'. In the noun form, it translates 'evangel' or 'gospel'.

Typical of the more than 130 times the word occurs in the New Testament is the angels' proclamation to the shepherds at Bethlehem: 'I bring you good news of great joy that will be for all the people. Today in the town of David a Saviour has been born to you; he is Christ the Lord' (Luke 2:10-11 NIV).

Speaking of the ministry of the coming Messiah, the prophet Isaiah says: 'The Spirit of the Sovereign LORD is on me, because the LORD has anointed me to preach good news to the poor. He has sent me to bind up the broken hearted, to proclaim freedom for the captives and release from darkness for the prisoners, to proclaim the year of the LORD's favour' (Isa. 61:1-2 NIV).

Jesus interpreted his mission as fulfillment of this promise (Luke 4:18–19). He saw himself as an evangelist, announcing the coming of the kingdom, and to 'do the will of God' who sent him (John 4:24). In him the gospel became flesh and dwelt among us (John 1:14). He was himself 'the way, the truth and the life' (John 14:6). For a few brief years, he assumed our likeness and showed us who God is and how much he cares. 'He took up our infirmities and carried our sorrows' (Isa. 53:4). At last, 'he bore our sins in his body' on the cross (1 Pet. 2:24); he suffered for us, 'the righteous for the unrighteous' (1 Pet. 3:18), that through his death the world might be saved.

Having effected forever our redemption through his blood, he rose from the grave 'according to the scriptures' (1 Cor. 15:3–4). He appeared to his disciples in his resurrected body, then ascended back into heaven whence he came. There in exalted reign, he ever lives 'to save completely those who come to God through him' (Heb. 7:25).

There is no other way – 'no other name under heaven given to men by which we must be saved' (Acts 4:12). Jesus offers himself as the only mediator between God and man. We may not fathom the mysteries of the Trinity, nor comprehend the scope of divine providence, but we can see Jesus. Simply pointing people to Jesus reminds me of William Taylor who, during the Gold Rush in California of the 19th century, went to San Francisco to evangelize. Having no church building, he went out on the streets to gather a congregation. He shouted to the passing crowd: 'What's the news?' Having arrested their attention, the evangelist began his message, 'Thank God, I have good news for you this morning, my brothers!' Then he proceeded to tell them of our God 'who so loved the world that he gave his one and only Son, that whoever believes in him shall not perish but have eternal life' (John 3:16).

All by Grace

Herein is the wonder of the gospel. It is not that we loved God, but that he loved us and gave himself for us, 'while we were still sinners' (Rom. 5:8). God accepted our judgement that we might receive his righteousness. It is all rooted in mercy. In our complete helplessness, God did for us what we could never do for ourselves. Contrary to the notions of a humanistic culture, the gospel does not disclose our search for God. Rather, it reveals God's undying quest for us. Everything about our salvation is initiated by divine grace.

That is why grace is so amazing. God does not ask us to lift ourselves out of the mire – he does it for us. Not because of our earnest toil and works of penance, but by His unmerited love alone he saves us, when in brokenness and repentance, by simple faith, we receive 'the gift of God' (Eph. 2:8).

The late Dr. Charles Berry, when he began his ministry, preached an inadequate gospel. Like many other young men who have gone through a liberal theological training, he questioned the saving efficacy of Christ's blood, and looked upon Jesus more as a great moral teacher than a divine Saviour. During his first pastorate in England, late one night while sitting in his study he heard a knock. Opening the door, he saw a girl standing.

'Are you a minister?' she asked. Getting an affirmative answer, she went on anxiously. 'You must come with me quickly; I want you to get my mother in.'

Imagining that it was a case of some drunken woman out on the streets, Berry said, 'Why, you must go and get a policeman.'

'No,' said the girl, 'my mother is dying, and you must come with me and get her in – to heaven.'

The young minister dressed and followed her. Let into the woman's room, he knelt beside her and began to describe the goodness and kindness of Jesus, explaining that he had come to show us how to live unselfishly. Suddenly the desperate woman cut him off. 'Mister,' she cried, 'that's no use for the likes of me. I am a sinner. Can't you tell me of someone who can have mercy upon me, and save my poor soul?'

'I stood there,' said Dr. Berry, 'in the presence of a dying woman, and I had nothing to tell her. In the midst of sin and death I had no message. . . . In order to bring something to that dying woman, I leaped back to my mother's knee, to my cradle faith, and told her the story of the cross and the Christ who was able to save to the uttermost.'

Tears began running over the cheeks of the eager woman. 'Now you are getting at it,' she said. 'Now you are helping me.'

And the famed preacher, concluding the story, said. 'I got her in, and blessed by God, I got in myself.'[2]

When we receive that gift of life, his Spirit begins to recreate us according to his own nature. God actually incorporates us into his body so that we become an extension of his body in the world. That which motivated our Lord's life now begins to constrain ours. The love of God is poured 'into our hearts by the Holy Spirit whom he has given us' (Rom. 5:5). His love is the fountain from which evangelism flows. It is not worked up, but released.

Everyone Must Hear

Coming from God, this love by its nature cannot be self-contained. The Father sent the Son to be 'the Saviour of the world' (John 4:42). God 'wants all men to be saved, and to come to a knowledge of the truth' (1 Tim. 2:4). The gospel invitation is addressed to all who will call upon the name of the Lord (Rom. 10:13). Anyone who repents of sin and comes to Christ in true faith shall be saved. God is no respecter of persons. Not everyone will believe the gospel, but everyone must hear.

With this assumption, it is not within our jurisdiction to make distinctions of privilege. We are under obligation to bring the good news 'both to Greeks and to non-Greeks, both to the wise and to the foolish' (Rom. 1:14). No social, racial, or cultural barriers can be raised against the preaching of redeeming grace. There is no biblical distinction between home and foreign missions. It is all world evangelism.

This will mean giving more attention to reaching persons who have a somewhat similar or completely diverse culture and language, and where there may be no viable church. Likely they live in out-of-the-way and distant places, but some will be found in our own cities and neighborhoods. Wherever they are, they need to be located, and their ways learned. Too long we have been cloistered in our ecclesiastical ghettos with no vision for the regions beyond. If the Great Commission is going to be fulfilled, we cannot place any limits on our responsibility to permeate the non-Christian world. Any method that will get the job done should be utilized.

However we go about it, let us persevere. Evangelism is an unceasing responsibility and privilege. Only when we see ourselves involved constantly in this witness are we living by the New Testament pattern. The more we become involved the more we feel the tug of a dying world. Everywhere bewildered and frightened people cry out for someone to care. They are lost – millions of them – their only certainty the grave. These are people for whom God gave his Son.

The Great Commission Lifestyle

Conversion is only the beginning of an ongoing process of learning whereby we are progressively conformed to the life of our Lord. We are not asked to make converts, but to 'make disciples' of all nations (Matt. 28:19). To this end we go, baptize and teach, just as in other versions of the command, we are sent, we preach and witness (John 17:18; 20:21; Mark 16:15; Luke 24:48; Acts 1:8). Only as disciples are made can these related activities find their purpose.[3]

Disciples continue to grow in the likeness of Jesus, and in so doing, they become involved in his ministry. In time, maturing disciples will begin to make disciples of others, teaching them in turn to do the same. Too often we have not kept this objective in mind, emphasizing spectacular numbers of people confessing Christ, with little subsequent concern for their holiness. We must recognize our responsibility to nurture new Christians in their priesthood.

Evangelism and discipleship complement each other. Neither can be healthy without the other. To stress only coming to Christ and neglect training eventually demeans the church by bringing in babies who do not grow. On the other hand, to emphasize education and neglect aggressive world outreach ultimately will stagnate the church by cutting off the flow of new life.

As disciples follow Christ their understanding of ministry grows. Every member of the church shares in the work of the body (Eph. 4:11-12; John 14:12). By virtue of different gifts, roles of ministry will vary, but all are servants. Disciples are made through relationships, especially with persons close to us. Like raising children, opportunities for mentoring surround us. Seizing these gives new meaning to every activity, as increasingly life is directed by the Great Commission. Nothing is insignificant.

Caring for the souls of persons brings an awakened social consciousness. We become more sensitive to the needs of the whole person – body, mind and soul. As resources permit, we do what we can to show the love of God. Infused into whatever form ministry takes is the outworking of Christ's purpose 'to seek and to save the lost' (Luke 19:10). Where this is not realized, an indispensable aspect of our Lord's life has yet to be learned.

Many of us may need to rearrange priorities in order to devote ourselves more lovingly to the world's need. Evangelism is costly. There is a cross in it – the daily offering up of ourselves to do the will of God.

Joy of the Harvest

One final aspect of evangelism must be mentioned – the joy that comes to those committed to this work. Jesus speaks of it as 'wages, bringing forth fruit for eternal life, so that the sower and the reaper may be glad together' (John 4:36). To know eternal life in Christ; to realize that you are a part of what God is doing to gather a people from the ends of the earth, a people made beautiful in holiness who will never cease to worship him – what more could you ask for?

Jesus lived with this vision, the 'joy set before him' which made the sufferings of the cross endurable (Heb. 12:2). He knows that as harvest workers multiplied the day was hastening when the gospel of the kingdom would be preached in all the world, and then he would return to reign over his people forever. He taught his disciples to live in this expectation – to view our work now in light of eternity.

John the beloved saw that final harvest when caught up in the Spirit on the isle of Patmos. Peering through the door of heaven, he beheld a great worshipping host. They are clothed in white robes and waving palm branches of victory. As far as the eye can see they are there from 'every nation, tribe, people and language' (Rev. 7:9). The Great Commission will be fulfilled! In the schedule of God it is already accomplished; the celebration has begun. Hallelujahs of the completed church are ringing through the streets of gold. A mighty voice can be heard, saying: 'Salvation to our God who sits on the throne, and to the Lamb' (Rev. 7:10).

Years ago in an expedition to an unreached area in India the Reverend E.P. Scott came upon a band of hostile warriors. They seized him, pointing their long spears at his heart. Feeling helpless, the old missionary drew out the violin which he had with him, put it to his shoulder, and began to play and sing in their native language:

> *All hail the power of Jesus' name!*
> *Let angels prostrate fall:*
> *Bring forth the royal diadem*
> *And crown him Lord of all!*

As the words rang out, Reverend Scott closed his eyes, momentarily expecting death. But when nothing happened, he opened his eyes. Spears had fallen from the hands of his captors. Tears filled their eyes. The warriors begged him to tell them of that Name – the Name above every other name, the Name by which everyone can come to God. So he went home with them, winning many to Christ, and raising up a church still rejoicing in salvation.[4]

Whatever may come, we know that the Name of Christ shall prevail. The certainty of that day establishes the vision which directs evangelism. The King is coming! While all that lies before us is not yet clear, 'we know that when he appears, we shall be like him, for we shall see him as he is' (1 John 3:2). Every knee shall bow before him and 'every tongue confess that Jesus Christ is Lord' (Phil. 2:11). At last our faith will turn to sight, and we will see the full extent of evangelism's reach.

Dr. Robert Coleman is Distinguished Professor of Evangelism and Discipleship at Gordon-Conwell Theological Seminary in South Hamilton, Mass., USA. He previously served as Director of the School of World Mission and Evangelism at Trinity International University. He ministers as an evangelist and teacher in various ways around the world.

---

[1] Much of this chapter has been taken from my books, *The Master's Way of Personal Evangelism* (Wheaton: Crossway, 1997); *The Heartbeat of Evangelism* (Colorado Springs: NavPress, 1985); *The Great*

Commission Lifestyle (Old Tappan: Fleming H. Revell, 1992); *The Mind of the Master* (Old Tappan: Fleming H. Revell, 1983); and *Evangelism in Perspective* (Camp Hill: Christian Publications, 1975).

2 Narrated by Paul Rees in an editorial in 'World Vision', Dec. 1971, p. 31.

3 The ramifications of this point are explored in my study of Christ's strategy of ministry in the gospels, *The Master Plan of Evangelism* (Old Tappan: Fleming H. Revell, 1963, 1964, 1993); and its sequel study of the local church in the Book of Acts, *The Master Plan of Discipleship* (Old Tappan: Fleming H. Revell, 1987, 1998).

4 Told by Louis Albert Banks, *Immortal Hymns and Their Stories* (Cleveland: Burrows Brothers, 1898), pp. 112-13; also see Amos R. Wells, 'All Hail the Power of Jesus Name', *The Christian Endeavor World*, May 26, 1904.

The Next Forty Years for Christian Missions

Patrick Johnstone

One of the greatest ways to stay on the cutting edge of world missions, is to be involved in evangelism yourself, especially with people from other lands who may live right in your midst. Beware of the struggles you will face as you launch into this: there will be failure; there will be disappointments. But remember that disappointment in evangelism can often be God's appointment to teach us something greater and something better.

George Verwer

The last forty years have been the most astonishing in missions history. Who could have foretold the amazing growth of the Church in the non-Western world, the penetration of the gospel to areas seemingly sealed off from God's messengers and the globalization of missions? Will the next forty years be as successful? Might it never be completed because our Returning King decides the task is done, the Bride is readied and time be no more?

This past forty years also represents the span of George Verwer's ministry – as well as my own! Think of some of the changes over these forty years and then project forward with me to the next forty to see what the world could look like if the same growth continued. I have picked six major facets in assessing the likelihood of this, and what we must do to either attain this or improve on it.

The Shift of Christianity to the non-Western World

For the Church's first 800 years there was a numerical balance between Western and non-Western Christians, but then followed a millennium in which Christianity was marginalized, suppressed, or even eliminated in nearly every part of the world except Europe. It is only in the last century that this has been reversed. In 1960 there were 672 million Western and only 370 million non-Western Christians, the latter being 35.5% of all Christians. By 2000 this had become 810 million and 1172 million, respectively (59%). By 2040, if the decline in the West and increase in non-West continues, this would become respectively 657 million and 1917 million (75%). What an extraordinary century of successful missionary endeavour this will have been! Will it happen? Only if we, as the Church, direct enormous effort at the following:

1. *Reverse the catastrophic effects of the Enlightenment in Europe* which has eroded the Christian heritage and worldview and emasculated its impact and witness. The West needs revival of those who are believers, renewal of traditional Christianity to make it relevant in a post-Christian, secular context and a massive ingathering of the millions who have had no vital contact with biblical Christianity.
2. *See massive breakthroughs in the major non-Christian religious blocs* – specifically the Muslims, Hindus and Buddhists. Growth has largely been among those not linked to these religions. This is a huge challenge for prayer, commitment and loving outreach to these 2.5 billion people, which without this will have increased to over 3.8 billion in 2040.
3. *Do far more to reach children and young people.* We face a spiritual disaster unless more effort is made to retain the next generation for Christ and make them effective disciples. Blinded by recent successes in making a first generation to be Christians, we have not realized that this will disappear in two generations if we do not disciple the rising generation.

The Triumph of Evangelicalism

The staggering nature of the modern Evangelical Awakening has not fully dawned on many. The decline of Christendom in the

West has obscured a massive growth of evangelicals in nearly every part of the world. Mainline Protestant denominations seduced by liberal theology are in massive decline or becoming evangelical. Roman Catholics are in disarray, lacking priests, nuns and missionaries, and discredited by huge paedophile scandals. Orthodox Churches are grasping for political leverage to survive. Evangelicals have taken centre stage in the Christian world – often with increased persecution.

Gains by evangelicals in the West are marginal to modest, but in the non-West are generally massive. In global terms we estimate evangelicals to have numbered 85 million, or 2.8% of the world's population in 1960, and forty years later this to have risen to 420 million (6.9%), which is a five-fold increase. With growth trends of the past forty years continuing for the next forty we could have 1,360 million evangelicals (15%) in a three-fold increase. Many challenges have to be met if we are to go on growing and advancing:

1. *A clear focus on world evangelization.* This can so easily be dissipated with a multiplicity of secondary goals and the momentum lost. The AD 2000 and Beyond Movement was one of the most successful global mobilization initiatives of history. The many spin-off visionary movements generated locally and regionally have significantly extended the outreach of the Church to the less evangelized. A clear focus in the succeeding generation has yet to emerge.

2. *Disunity and fragmentation are real possibilities on cultural, ethnic, doctrinal, financial and personal grounds.* Is this one reason that increased levels of persecution have been allowed by God during the successful 1990s to keep us dependent and humble? The future for world evangelization is dependent on a level of partnering hitherto unknown that will bridge differences in our globalizing world.

3. *A lack of biblical discipling.* Outreach and church-planting have not resulted in many discipled Christians or sufficient godly leaders. The evident lack of motivation and mobilization of most Evangelicals is unfortunately too obvious. Are we going to disciple the next generation in our churches? Without them all thought of continued growth is but a dream.

Empires Past and Future

World War II was the trigger for a massive dismantling of empires: German, Japanese, French, British, Portuguese and Soviet. Massive political change, rising ethnic consciousness and globalization have impacted everyone and made them more receptive to spiritual change. The 1989 tearing down of the Berlin Wall not only signi-fied the end of Russian Communist hegemony, but also the end of 200 years of ideological dominance which began with the French Revolution in 1789. This was followed by a decade of extraordinary openness, even greater church growth, increased persecution and the spread of electronic communications. The decade of single-superpower dominance ended with the Islamist attack on the USA on September 11, 2001.

The empires of the 21st century will be different and less tangible:

1. US cultural and economic dominance will probably persist until 2040.
2. Islamic expansionism through oil wealth, migration, subtle and less-subtle threats to non-Islamic societies often distorting cultures and legal systems to favour Islam.
3. Chinese influence through industrialization, massive population size and export of its excesses legally and illegally and the growth of the overseas Chinese communities in virtually every nation of the world. By 2040 China's economic and political muscle could be a major geopolitical force.

How will this affect Christian ministry? Few realize the extraor-dinary worldview changes that came to Christianity around AD 310 when Emperor Constantine declared Christianity the religion of the Roman Empire. Biblical patterns of leadership, living with persecution, godly lifestyles, worship, conversion and evangelism disappeared and were replaced by a tie-up with political systems, power politics, ecclesiastic empires, division between clergy and laity, formalism without need for conversion and so on. The great challenge is to recognize this and be willing to return to princi-ples of biblical Christianity, but in 21st century clothing. The Church must radically change or go under. What are the indica-tions of this inexorable process?

1. The rapid marginalization of a Christian worldview and presence in the media and centres of power and influence.
2. The huge decline in commitment and numbers in mainline or traditional streams of Christianity.
3. The huge increase in non-traditional church structures, movements and networks over the past 50 years. The only Christian mega-bloc that has grown massively is that of Independent or Indigenous Christianity. These movements owe little to, and know less of, historic Christianity.
4. The surge in levels of persecution – whether from Hindu extremists, Islamists, Asian Marxists or Western Secularists.

Are Christians entering a new era where the Church becomes a despised, hated, persecuted minority, yet thereby freed from being a kingdom of this world as a committed, purified, incisive and a relevant alternative society that attracts multitudes? We should prepare for world evangelization in the light of these trends. Some areas of focus to be effective:

1. *Ecclesiology.* We have been hampered by distorted ecclesiologies where the Great Commission was ignored or marginalized. This God-given Commission must be the centre of the life of the Church.
2. *Embrace the commitment needed for advance.* To be a missionary is going to be more risky and not be a soft option.
3. *A great faith in God that He is in control.* The very changes and upheavals which the world is experiencing are the means by which God is going to open up hard areas, peoples and individuals to the gospel.

Unreached Peoples Still Need to be Reached

In 1960 only a few missions were thinking in terms of peoples rather than countries, and no one knew how many peoples there were. David Barrett had only begun on his listing of Africa's peoples in what became the fundamental list of peoples for derivations by others and only finally published in the *World Christian Encyclopedia* in 2001. Wycliffe Bible Translators had brought out the *Ethnologue* in 1951 which, for the first time, listed all known languages of the world. *Operation World* helped to make Christians more aware of peoples within countries, stimulating more prayer. Then came the efforts of MARC-World Vision, and the clarion call of Ralph Winter at the Lausanne Congress in 1974 to do something about the world's 'Hidden Peoples'.

This led to a large-scale increase in people awareness, years of work in defining our terms and listing all the world's peoples. This made the Joshua Project listing of least-reached peoples possible in 1995. We ended the century not only with virtually completed lists for the whole world, but many national surveys of peoples with a reasonable analysis of who and where the least reached were. This culminated with the effort of the AD 2000 and Beyond Movement to encourage churches and mission agencies to adopt peoples for prayer and ministry. By the end of 2000 only a few hundred of the peoples over 10,000 population remained unadopted. We enter the 21st century with the task of analysis and adoption of peoples within sight of being achieved. What is there left to do?

1. *Around 3,000 of the 12,000 ethno-linguistic peoples are still a pioneer challenge,* but the number of peoples without a single believer or mission agency seeking to reach them has fallen to probably less than 1,000. More research needs to be done to better understand their spiritual neediness, need of the Scriptures, and required investment of resources.

2. *The countries with mega-challenges for unreached peoples* are Chad in Africa, China and Indonesia's many unreached minority peoples. The largest and most complex challenge of all is India with divisions along caste lines as well as language, religion and ethnicity. Our ability to complete the discipling of the world's peoples to a great extent depends on how we face up to the challenge of India.

3. *The continuing need for Bible translation.* No people can be adequately discipled without the Scriptures in their heart language. In 1960 there were possibly eight hundred languages with a portion of Scriptures. Over the subsequent forty years, largely through the efforts of the Bible Societies and WBT/SIL over 2,000 languages were added to this total. Successful Bible

translations have actually done more to preserve the viability and use of smaller languages than any other single factor, but over the twenty-first century it is estimated that over half of the present 7,000+ languages will die out. There are possibly 2,000 languages still needing to be translated, and another 2,000 which need to be further analysed to see if a Bible translation is a viable project.

The Discrediting of Religious Ideologies

In 1960 Communism threatened world conquest. Islam, Hinduism, Buddhism and Christendom itself appeared entrenched. How changed this appeared in 2000! The vast majority of those not yet evangelized are Muslim, Hindu and Buddhist. All three religions claim to have received revelations that are universally applicable, and have holy books to codify their beliefs. All three have been invigorated by interactions with Christianity and developed 'missions' to Christian countries – Muslim missionaries, New Age proponents of Hindu philosophies and the Dalai Lama's promotion of Buddhism.

Islam

Very little direct outreach to Muslims was done in 1960. The few Muslims who had come to faith in Christ were isolated from their own societies and often not welcomed in Christian communities. Muslims appeared too hard for God.

In 1965 came the massive growth of Christianity in Indonesia with possibly millions of, admittedly very nominal, Muslims coming to Christ. Other significant movements to Christ from Islam began to occur in Bangladesh, Nigeria, Algeria, Central Asia, Bosnia, among Iranians and so on. Massive increase in prayer for the Muslim world, a great increase in the number of long-term missionaries committed to specifically Muslim outreach, and disillusionment with Islam (both with the venality and oppression of Muslim leaders and the extremism of Islamists) have contributed to this. All around the Muslim world, Muslim background believers' groups are developing and growing.

Almost everywhere that an extreme Islamist movement has either come to power (as in Iran, Sudan, Afghanistan) or has initiated a war of terror (Egypt, Algeria, Indonesia) the number of those coming to Christ has increased. The terrorist attack on the USA on 11 September, 2001 has radically changed perceptions in and about Islam. 'Moderate' Muslim leaders have not adequately defined their theological rejection of terrorist action for, at its heart, Islam is committed to world conquest by violence if necessary. Many Muslims are more open to reconsider their allegiance to Islam than ever before. We need to recruit, prepare, equip and deploy a new generation of workers with a heart for bringing Muslims to Jesus.

Hinduism

In India the majority of the least reached communities are those enmeshed in the caste system of Hinduism. The higher the caste status, the lower the response to the gospel has been. The rise of nationalistic and fascist movements has shattered religious harmony. Extremist groups had great influence in the BJP government of 2000 and which has sheltered their violent suppression of Muslims and increased persecution of Christians. This has both discredited Hinduism among the many who are more moderate and stirred a massive protest from the Dalit.

During 2001 Dalit anger at centuries of oppression and the recent rise in Hindu extremism has led to a growing movement to renounce all links with Hinduism and openly espouse another religion such as Buddhism, Islam or Christianity. It is possible that 300 million people could change their religion over the next ten to fifteen years and that, despite skewed legislation which discriminates against Christians, many could also become followers of the Lord Jesus. The latter possibility will depend much on how Christians respond to this challenge and open their doors to a flood of new Christians. The social and spiritual implications of this are huge. India must have a very high priority in our prayers and Christian involvement over the next forty years, for it is on the northern plains of India that the largest concentration of the unreached are to be found.

Buddhism

I well remember in 1979 when ministering with the MV *Logos* in Colombo, Sri Lanka, we met many Buddhist priests. Some proudly boasted of the superiority of Buddhism, claiming, 'We do not kill people like you Christians do.' That was shortly before the terrible Hindu Tamil–Buddhist Sinhala civil war; Buddhist priests were at the forefront. It is not surprising that since then the decline in Christianity in Sri Lanka was halted and thousands have come to a living faith in Christ.

The Buddhist culture of Thailand is being rocked by scandals of immorality and corruption among the clergy. In many countries the long-established Buddhist order has been upset, and a new openness to Christianity come. Even Tibetans, long one of the hardest Buddhist ethnic groups are now beginning to respond and the first indigenous Tibetan churches are being formed.

These religious systems *are* a challenge, but we have seen enough of God's working over the last forty years to trust him for the breakthroughs among these religions which cannot give hope and assurance of salvation.

Mobilization of Missionaries

In 1960 the mission force was white, western and respected. They went to the field on ships and usually single and often stayed for the rest of their working life on the field. Short-term missionaries were almost unknown. In 2000 the mission force had become global but no longer unquestioningly respected, often needing to hide their identity from kidnappers, secret police, hostile governments, curious reporters and even uninformed Christians. They go to the field first as short-termers by plane, and their overseas ministry can be just one phase in a multi-faceted career.

In 1960 English-speaking USA, UK, Canada and Australasia provided the vast majority of missionaries. Now Koreans, Chinese, Filipino, Indian and Portuguese-speaking Brazilians are major components of the world's mission force. In the late 1990s Korea became the world's second-largest sender of foreign missionaries, overtaking the UK. The Asian component of the 201,000 missionaries identified in the 2001 *Operation World* was 35%, just behind that of North America at 36%.

The major change in Western sending patterns is the explosion of short-term mission interest ranging from two-week field visits to one- or two-year terms of service. Long-term mission numbers have remained constant or are in slight decline. The number of home staff has more than doubled, demonstrating that in order to maintain the vital long-term mission force a huge investment in personnel to recruit, train, pastor a growing army of short-termers must be made.

The major change in global missions is the removal of barriers of distance and communication between local churches and fields. This is increasing the direct sending of missionaries (with mixed results), increased impatience with mission agencies and many more field visits by local church leadership.

What of the future? Note the following:

1. *The globalization of missions will continue.* Missions will have to be multi-cultural in composition or in field partnering. Much greater sensitivity to multiple missionary cultures as well as target cultures will be an essential component of training and orientation on the field.
2. *Partnering is the future of missions.* The concept of the lone pioneer has gone. We cannot do it alone as agencies, nationalities, churches or denominations.
3. *Mission agencies will have to adapt to the local church* desire for hands-on involvement and a greater say in policy.
4. *The limitations and costs of short-term missions need to be watched,* and all short-term programs evaluated for their value-added contribution to the overall goal of world evangelization.

Conclusion

We face a challenging future, yet we can do this with hope. The God who has led and sustained the advances of the past forty years will do the same for the next forty years – but only if we follow in faith! May the next forty years be an even greater testimony to God's grace and power!

Patrick Johnstone served in southern Africa with the Dorothea Mission for sixteen years as a tent evangelist and Bible translator. During this time he wrote the first of six editions of Operation World. *In 1978 Patrick and his wife Jill left Africa and served for one year on OM's ship* Logos.  *In 1980 they commenced ministry with WEC International as part of the leadership team and responsible for strategy and research. In 1992 Jill died. Patrick married Robyn in 1995. In 2002 they handed over to successors both their WEC leadership role and the writing of* Operation World. *They continue with WEC in a wider ministry of speaking, writing and teaching. Patrick also authored* The Church Is Bigger Than You Think *in 1998.*

Section 4

Words of Tribute

Incurable Fanatic – Unshakeable Friend

Peter Conlan

They charge me with fanaticism. If to be feelingly alive to the sufferings of my fellow creatures is to be a fanatic, I am one of the most incurable fanatics ever permitted to be at large.

William Wilberforce, Slave Abolitionist,
British House of Commons, June 19th, 1816

The Oxford English Dictionary defines a fanatic as 'a person filled with excessive enthusiasm, especially in religion'. Non-conformist Christians were called 'fanatics' two hundred years ago. Later they were known as 'enthusiasts' and by the mid-20th century they had been quietly absorbed into the religious mainstream.

In February 1962 Britain's evangelical quietness was shattered with a cry for 'spiritual revolution' from a very thin and very intense young American called George Verwer. He was immediately labelled a fanatic and good Christian parents and ministers were advised to lock up their young.

One report in the British Christian press said, '*George Verwer is a self-confessed fanatic! He is also a revolutionist, and a Christian. It may be considered unusual to find these three characteristics in one person, but then, George Verwer is a most unusual person.*'

This 'fanatic' has been my mentor and one of my closest friends for more than thirty-five years. During our first meeting in Bromley, Kent, as a young Christian I admitted to so many spiritual struggles and questions that any normal mission agency would have rejected me outright. George immediately gave me a handful of books to read overnight and an invitation not to join OM but to join him – 'starting from tomorrow'. Six weeks later I was typing his letters in a humid, cockroach-infested flat in Bombay, India.

The months that followed, criss-crossing India by train, truck and plane with George, challenged and changed my life. George is always interesting but not always easy. My task was to book our travel tickets, usually with instructions to purchase the fastest and cheapest possible. I once failed to book the fastest train from Bombay to Bangalore. Our slower train *followed* the 'Bangalore Express' and George was not pleased. Half way there, at Guntakal Junction, we slid to a halt where we remained perspiring in unbearable heat for the next few hours. The *Grace Awakening*, like our train, had not yet arrived, and George was visibly irritated. Then word arrived from further down the track explaining our delay. The 'Bangalore Express' had crashed resulting in many fatalities. George's immediate tears of compassion were mixed with prayers of thanksgiving to God for His sovereignty in our travel arrangements!

As a single OM worker I lived with the ever-active George and ever-patient Drena, in India, Nepal, Thailand, England and on board the old *Logos*. My wife, Birgitta, and I shared the same house in England with George and Drena for five years. I have seen George at his best and his worst. We have laughed together until we have ached, sometimes in a church meeting naively hoping no one would notice. We have prayed and wept together – he far more than I – over the disappointments and heartbreaks and hurts in Christian ministry. For thirty-five years I have seen no gap between the man and the message; no difference between the public George Verwer and the private George Verwer. He is for real.

The tributes that follow will express better than I the global scale of George's impact upon missions. But in true Verwer style I have six words that are for me the real George:

Brokenness

There's a place on the old Silk Road between Istanbul and Ankara where our friendship almost ended. It was 1968, we were both young men, and I was driving a VW van packed with the Verwer family and team. Everyone was tired, thirsty and hungry. George was impatient to keep pressing on. I eventually slammed the brakes on and shouted to George to get out. To the stunned amazement of the team George and I faced each other with clenched fists. I said to George, 'go on, Christian leader, hit me!' For a moment we glared at each other and I waited for impact. Then George began to shake, tears started to flow and his arms were wrapped around my shoulders. Brokenness at the foot of the cross is not only his message, it is his life.

Gentleness

February 1968, on the dried up banks of the river Pampa, near Kozhencherry, in Kerala, South India, 80,000 people gathered under a straw-roofed *pandal*. The Maramon Convention is the largest Christian conference in the world. Speakers have included, Dr. E. Stanley Jones and Sadhu Sundar Singh. That year George was a guest speaker – the biggest preaching engagement of his life – and I was to be his practical helper. The night before the great event I went down with a malarial fever. As I drifted in and out of consciousness, George sat with me throughout the night, gently mopping me down with a wet cloth. Years later I witnessed that same gentleness, as he fed his aged father who was shaking uncontrollably with advanced Parkinson's disease. The Fruit of the Spirit has always underpinned George's ministry.

Recklessness

The truth is we knew very little about ships, but after five years of prayer for the ship project, *Now was the Hour for the Ship*. August 1969 I walked into George's office and he handed me an air ticket. 'I want you to go to Athens to meet with Aristotle Onassis to see if he has a suitable ship for us.' I replied that I knew nothing about buying ships. George handed me a book on the life of Onassis and said, 'Read this on the plane!' A reckless faith in God and an amazing belief in people sets George's leadership apart.

Uniqueness

Not many preachers prepare sermons like George does. Often he will furiously scribble a few key words on a scrap of paper moments before getting up to preach. His unique hieroglyphics are almost never written on a blank sheet of paper. I have seen his sermon notes scrawled over the cover of magazines, church bulletins, old memos and even on the back of travel documents. George's real sermon preparation takes place on his knees. At a major OM conference one evening years ago, he and I were in a back room just minutes before he was due to preach. 'Conlan, I have no idea what to preach on tonight. You find the text, I'm going to pray.' Moments later he stood before many hundreds of young people and solemnly announced his text. It was only as George began struggling through a very obscure passage in 1 Samuel that I realised my mistake. It should have been 2 Samuel! I rushed up to the pulpit and handed him the correct reference. Without missing a beat he announced the new text and preached with power and anointing. George is of course unique but his dependence upon God keeps the spotlight where he wants it.

Loyalty

George has few acquaintances, only friends. I know of no other Christian leader who personally keeps in touch by phone and correspondence with so many people. To be a friend of George's is to be a friend for life. The testimony of many OM co-workers, pastors, missionaries and leaders on the edge of despair is the same – 'George's phone call restored hope and belief.'

In 1995 OM experienced the biggest financial blow in our history. We, along with scores of other Christian agencies, were deceived by George's old friend, Jack Bennett, Jr., the head of the New Era Philanthropy Foundation. Bennett was subsequently sentenced to twelve years in Federal prison for carrying out what experts believe is the biggest charity fraud case in American history.

Christmas Day, 1998, I received a call from George. His scratchy phone voice yelled out, 'Merry Christmas!' I asked 'Where are you?' He replied, 'I'm in prison visiting one of my dearest friends.' George was visiting Jack Bennett, the man who had defrauded OM of one million dollars (funds eventually recovered in the overall settlement). For George the 'revolution of love' is more than a slogan, it is loyalty and commitment for life.

Prayer

Thirty years ago George sent me on my first line-up assignment for the old *Logos* ship, to East Africa. He personally typed a note of misspelled instructions and before I walked down the gangway he said 'Let's pray.'

I called him two weeks ago hours before I flew out to Havana, Cuba, on the latest line-up assignment for OM Ships. Before putting the phone down George said, 'Let's pray'. If there is only one word to explain the secret of George's enormous impact it is prayer. He has simply made prayer his life's priority.

Postscript

This morning's post included a hand-written note from George. It was scribbled in his unique scrawl on recycled paper. His note ended,

> *You have been a great friend and a huge encouragement over 35 years.*
> *Thank you,*
> *George*
> *PS. Your wife is a jewel*

So, George Verwer, incurable fanatic and my unshakeable friend,

> *You have been a great friend and a huge encouragement over 35 years.*
> *Thank you,*
> *Peter*
> *PS. Your wife is a jewel*

Peter Conlan has served with OM in many parts of the world for more than thirty-five years. He is with the OM Ships leadership team and is a member of the Board of Directors for Logos II. *His more recent responsibilities have included co-ordinating the ship visits to China, Vietnam and*  Burma. *Peter's busy speaking ministry enables him to function as a sort of OM ambassador in many nations. He and his wife, Birgitta, reside in Bromley, UK. They have three lovely daughters, Esther, Helen and Anna.*

★ ★ ★ ★

When the history of contemporary
missions is recorded, the name of
George Verwer will be writ large. His
ability to enthuse the unenthusiastic,
mobilise the immobile, motivate the
unmotivated, comfort the afflicted and
afflict the comfortable is without parallel. His searing vision, relentless
energy, and iron determination in a
lesser man would have ridden roughshod over the less gifted
and the motivationally deficient. But his magnanimous spirit,
humble attitude, spiritual integrity, genuine love for people and
willingness to learn saved him from such destructive excess
and matured him into a leader people love to follow. We thank
God for him.

Stuart Briscoe, Pastor,
Elmbrook Church
USA

★ ★ ★ ★

Birds fly, but eagles soar. To soar is not just
to fly, but to fly high, to mount up with
speed and agility; be at a great height
above earth or above normal position. To
soar is to hover or sail in the air without
flapping of wings or use of engine. Where
eagles coast ordinary birds dare not
approach.

Birds fly high because they have big
hearts. The bigger the hearts the higher the flight. Flying gives
birds both competitive and perspective advantages. Great and
enviable though flying is, it is nothing compared to soaring.

This is my simple description of George. You have defied age,
culture, status, and distance. You have encouraged us who know
you to keep soaring high. Even when you are tired on those
jumbo jets, instead of sleeping, you write encouraging notes to us.

Keep on soaring dear brother – you were born an eagle!
God bless you and Drena.

Mrs. Judy W. Mbugua,
Director, Pan African Christian Women's Alliance
Nairobi

★ ★ ★ ★

The name "Jorge" brings to my mind someone who, hardly over twenty years old, indelibly marked my life for the future. Later, having launched other ministries independent of OM such as Misión Alturas ('Heights' Mission), one can see the footprints of Jorge and OM.

I always remember the values of the Word that he emphasized: prayer, warfare, forsaking all, victory. I have grounded myself in them over the years and I sincerely thank God for the teaching of the Word and quality of life of my brother Jorge.

Daniel González, Director, Alturas Mission, Spain
Linked with OM from the early 1960s until the late 1990s.

★ ★ ★ ★

I first met George Verwer at Urbana '87. I watched him as he communicated a global vision to more than 20,000 young people who sat in rapt attention as he spoke. He believes that the whole world must be reached with the gospel and there are no social or political barriers that he will recognize as interfering with the task of reaching the far corners of the earth with the message of Christ.

Perhaps the thing that most impresses me is his embracing of the simple lifestyle. He refuses to spend any money on himself other than what is essential for his survival. He is living simply so that others might simply live. He has given his all to the Master. He is someone who attempts great things for God and expects great things from God. It has been said, 'The strong obey when a strong man shows them the way.' This is a strong man who has chartered a path that strong young men and women over the last several decades have willingly followed even as he followed Christ.

Tony Campolo
Eastern University
St. David's, PA, USA

★ ★ ★ ★

We got to know George in 1961 when Kees and I were studying at Brussels Bible Institute. In the many years that we worked together with George, we learned to integrate lots of the principles he taught us into our lives. Among them were: love for this world in need; the importance of prayer; transparency in our relationships and immediate repentance.  The most important matter about our relationship with George, however, is that, even after we left OM years ago, George remains a very wonderful and faithful friend, who has encouraged and helped us through phone calls, letters and visits throughout life. Thanks, George, for your friendship!

Toos Rosies
Toos, conference speaker and author of Polished but not Perfect, *served with OM from 1962 to 1985 in Holland and Belgium and in OM's conference ministries.*

★ ★ ★ ★

My first contact with George Verwer was under duress! Thirty years ago a persistent church member pestered me to invite him to my conservative church pulpit. I never regretted it. In one sermon he caused us to think globally and changed my strategy as a pastor. 'Verwer' and world vision are almost synonymous.

George has an almost unique ability to
inspire people to co-operate with him in
birthing his many schemes for the evangelisation of the cosmos. Equally vital, though
not so well known, is his pastoral heart that
has encouraged and envisioned so many.
Thousands have received his letters. Broken
leaders have known his balm, exhausted
missionaries have been rejuvenated, suc-

cessful business people have seen how vital they are to the Kingdom.

George is a man of many parts. I have watched him weep and
laugh. I have heard him preach outstanding sermons and listened
to him as a jet lagged individual try to cope. I have witnessed his
walk in faith marvelling at what God can do with an imperfect
man who dares to be different. Deservedly he has won the
respect of Christians around the world. One of the great privi-
leges in my life has been to know George Verwer and to call him
my friend.

Tony Sargent
Principal International Christian College Glasgow
Former pastor, Worthing Tabernacle, Sussex, UK

★ ★ ★ ★

George is a challenger. When he said to
me, 'Pray about going down to Mexico,'
and I asked what it would cost, he said,
'It'll cost you your life.' When he invited
me to an all night prayer meeting, I wondered what on earth anybody could pray
about the whole night. We confessed sin
and prayed over a world map and are still
seeing answers to those prayers. He's a
communicator, preaching to thousands,

but zealously follows up individuals by phone and letters. I appre-
ciate his message and vision as my own. He lives his faith and has
seen God do the extraordinary in our world.

Richard F. Griffin
Serving with OM in Mexico since 1958.

★ ★ ★ ★

George and Drena, I salute you on this
extraordinary occasion. Extraordinary
for one to step aside from a burgeon-
ing ministry he himself established. As
we commemorate the legacy of a
leader who pioneered the great movement of short-term missions, I consider it extraordinary because you held
the course in focusing short-term
ministry on long-term impact. And it's remarkable that a man
could lead so dynamic a movement and at the same time
preach 400 times a year and keep in personal touch with thousands of individuals! I count myself honored to be among
them, and celebrate one of my prime heroes by giving thanks
to God for His faithfulness to you and through you both.

Robertson McQuilkin
President Emeritus, Columbia International University
Columbia, South Carolina, USA

★ ★ ★ ★

I have known George since the Fall of
1958, when we were fated to study
together at Moody Bible Institute.
Perhaps my fates then were not favoured
in my way, because I had to sit next to
him in alphabetical order in the personal evangelism class. Life is never fair,
even in 1958. But in God's flowing
mercy, for forty-four years we have been
in relationship, generally separated by geography but closer in spir-
it and passion.

One gripping memory stands out in recent years, and it was a
very serious personal and missiological conversation we had in
what a friend dubbed 'The Chapel'. But this sacred space was none
other than a Kuala Lumpur hotel sauna, and there we sat one

steamy evening, sharing our hearts, encouraging one another, and using a dress code that Adam would have preferred prior to the Fall! This is what I call authentic and transparent contextualization!

What I admire most about George is his steady vision, his capacity to give away ministry and position, and his unwavering commitment to the living God, to the Church and to the task of world evangelisation.

Bill Taylor
Executive Director, Missions Commission, World Evangelical Alliance
★ ★ ★ ★

GEORGE. There are not many leaders of churches or mission agencies for whom just the first name finds full recognition; much less 95% feeling appreciation and admiration! How did this happen to a man who for the first twenty years of his ministry adamantly refused to allow his photo to be taken for a magazine?

We were children of the sixties. We were extreme in our application of 'forsaking all that you have' to give everyone on earth a little knowledge of the Saviour. Yet is it not amazing that OM never had a 'falling away', or a 'split'? Nor have we heard of anyone who felt GEORGE 'lorded it over them', or even 'insisted on his own way'.

What was it about George that would cause me and my wife to cheerfully find our way with a team of fourteen recent graduates overland from Manchester to New Delhi in an old lorry from the junkyard when we felt called to the Arab world? We knew that George was hearing from the Lord in an era when nobody in our circles talked that way!

What was inculcated in us as OMers, that resulted in the majority of the major Indian mission agencies starting up SINCE the first OM team arrived Jan. 1, 1964? What of George's understanding of the Lord, His Word, and a biblical pattern of living got passed on in such a way that the majority of agencies in the IMA have ex-OMers as their leaders?!

There is an article in a book about Christian leaders which describes GEORGE as 'inspired'. I wrote to the editor to explain that GEORGE is not inspired; many of us are inspired, and even inspiring. GEORGE IS ANOINTED. There's a huge difference. But maybe even more significantly, what caused us to 'seek first His Kingdom' with all of our hearts was that GEORGE has been an Isaiah 66:2 man with 'a broken and contrite spirit who trembles at My Word'.

Affectionately,
Greg Livingstone
Kuala Lumpur

Dr. Greg (and Sally) Livingstone was the first US Coordinator of OM, and took the first OM team to India. Always generous with his staff, George Verwer encouraged Livingstone to become the North American Director of Arab World Ministries in 1977. From 1983 to 2000 Livingstone served as General Director of Frontiers.

★ ★ ★ ★

After hitch-hiking from France to Madrid, Spain, in 1961, I met George, with the first OM team to Europe. He spoke to me about Jesus and gave me Billy Graham's *Peace with God*. I gave my life to Jesus and immediately joined the team.

Life with George was full of challenges: eating only bread and olives every day, sleeping on the office floor, travelling in old vehicles, praying for an impossible 300, then 1,000 young people for the first summer outreaches. Unforgettable was when George stood with Federico Aparisi and said, 'Look at us. We may let you down. Look at Jesus, He will never!' George's life, living out biblical principles, has impacted me permanently.

Drena is amazing. Living and travelling with her and the babies, I saw her willingness and obedience to the Lord, in spite of many struggles. With Galatians 6:9

Christa Eicher
Christa (nee Fischer) Eicher was with George and Drena 1961–62,
Turkey 1963–64, then OM India 1964–94. She and Ray live in
Mussoorie, North India

★ ★ ★ ★

Dear George and Drena
    We want to congratulate you upon your
years of leadership and vision given to
Operation Mobilisation. God did such a
masterful work in bringing a brash high
school kid to Christ through the prayers of
a dear lady and the evangelistic efforts of
Billy Graham.
    We are confident that without your lov-
ing partnership with George, Drena, that the overall ministry of
Operation Mobilisation would have been weakened.
    . . . Every association we have had with you and Opera-
tion Mobilisation has been a blessing. Please keep on keeping
on!!

John Kyle
Former Director, InterVarsity Missions, Senior Vice President,
Evangelical Fellowship of Mission Agencies, Atlanta

★ ★ ★ ★

My first training for missions was with
Operation Mobilisation. I applied to many
missions but was turned down by all, but in
the 1960s OM accepted anyone! I had the
wonderful opportunity of serving in India
from 1966 to 1968. George was a challenge
and encouragement to me in my walk with
God and zeal for His glory among the
nations. Many years later during surgery,
radiation, and chemotherapy for cancer, George was one of the
first to call to encourage and pray for me and sacrificially give
to assist with expenses. What a gracious, caring, kind man of
God!

Doug Nichols
International Director
Action International Ministries
Mountlake Terrace, Washington, USA

★ ★ ★ ★

The great George Verwer did not look very impressive. A new OMer in 1967 attending an OM training conference, I got up late at night. Walking through the dark hallway I stumbled on somebody: George Verwer. He was sleeping on a *coir* mat, no carpet below, no sheet, his mail scattered around him. This made such an impression on my heart of this international leader.

What kept us in OM was George's commitment. At the end of a conference in Patna he poured out his heart and said if it were possible he would cut off his hands and feet and give them to us. We knew he meant every word of that. This commitment and love built the leaders for India.

In 1982, when OM's Bombay office was burnt up, I took the blame, convinced that I should resign and was disqualified to be a leader. George spoke to me for more than half an hour over the phone, helped me to get over the guilt and pain and to press on for God. In 1989, another crisis hit me the likes of which I have never experienced in my life, and I wanted to quit the ministry. Again it was George who spoke to me, encouraged me, wrote to me, even screamed at me to get through to me, so that I would get over the pain and agony. Like me there are thousands who have gone through pain and agony who have been rejected, whom George has restored and helped to press on for Jesus Christ.

OM India would never have been what it is today if it was not for George's commitment to work in India and to the leaders in India. Hundreds and hundreds of people are even now praying for George and there are so many, literally, little 'George Verwers' all over, especially in Andhra Pradesh. These children have not been named 'George', but 'George Verwer'. So George Verwer will continue to live on . . . for the next generations.

AE 'Alfy' Franks
Managing Trustee
Operation Mobilisation India